GW01142455

Abu Dhabi

VISITORS' GUIDE

there's more to life...
askexplorer.com

'ERRARI WORLD ABU DHABI

'he world's first indoor Ferrari branded heme park, featuring its record breaking oller coaster, Formula Rossa which speeds p to 240 kmph.

ROOMS WITH ISLAND VIEW

Yas Island offers a great range of accommodation (from affordable to luxury) with Yas Viceroy and six centralized Yas Plaza hotels, all hosting gourmet restaurants, entertainment, fitness and wellness venues.

JNIQUE WATER ADVENTURES AT YAS WATERWORLD

The largest Emirati themed waterpark in the JAE and the world's first aqua park with a ollercoaster ride.

YAS LINKS GOLF COURSE

The first championship links course in the UAE designed by Kyle Phillips, a world leading golf course designer.

PURE RELAXATION – YAS BEACH

Let your soul wander, swim, paddle board, or kayak away on the shores of Yas Island's exclusive beach.

HOME TO THE FORMULA 1™ ETIHAD AIRWAYS ABU DHABI GRAND PRIX

Drive a Formula Yas 3000 or Aston Martin GT4 on the same circuit as the pros. – You can!

WHEREVER IN THE WORLD YOU HAVE COME FROM, WE'LL HELP YOU DISCOVER OURS.

From casual visitors to heads of government, InterContinental Abu Dhabi has welcomed guests from all over the world. So, we understand that people want much more than room and board. They want experiences that enrich and reward. That's why we offer a range of insider packages designed to connect our guests to the real Abu Dhabi and create lasting memories.

Do you live an InterContinental life?

For further information or to make a reservation
please call +971 2 666 6888
intercontinentalabudhabi.com
dining-intercontinental-ad.ae

INTERCONTINENTAL.
ABU DHABI

In over 170 locations across the globe including HONG KONG • LONDON • NEW YORK • PARIS

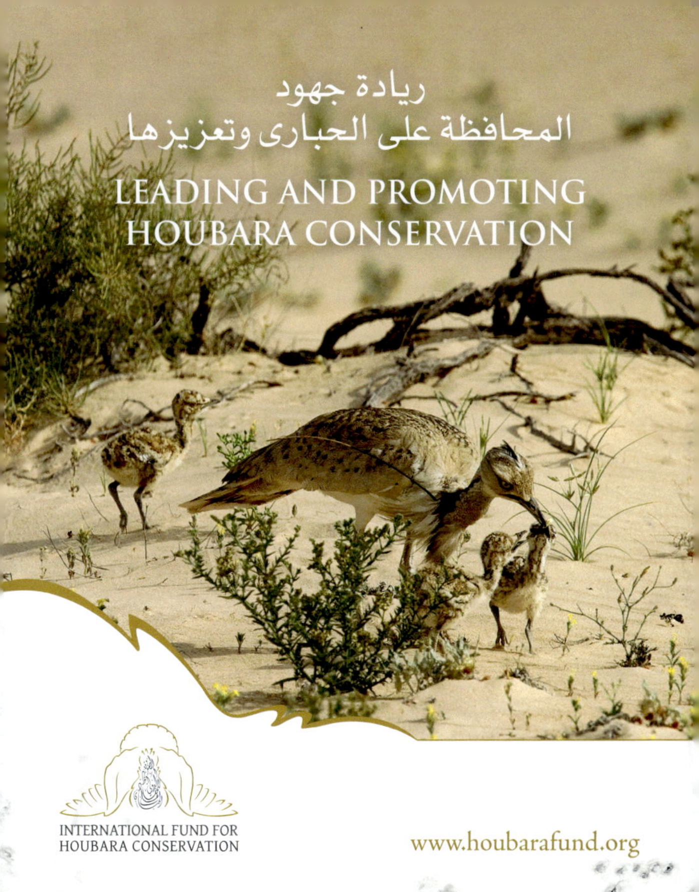

INTERNATIONAL FUND FOR
HOUBARA CONSERVATION

www.houbarafund.org

Abu Dhabi Visitors' Guide
ISBN – 978-9948-20-262-2

Front cover photograph: Hardy Mendrofa – Sheikh Zayed Grand Mosque

Explorer Publishing & Distribution
PO Box 34275, Dubai, United Arab Emirates
Phone (+971 4) 340 8805 Fax (+971 4) 340 8806
info@askexplorer.com
askexplorer.com

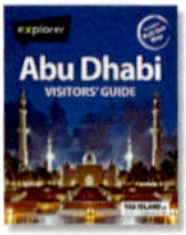

Welcome...

Welcome to the *Abu Dhabi Visitors' Guide.* This mini marvel has been passionately prepared by the same team that brought you the *Abu Dhabi Residents' Guide.* Written by local residents, and perfect for visitors, you'll find all you need to make the most out of your time in this interesting emirate – whether you're looking for the top restaurants, the most stylish shops or the best cultural spots.

Abu Dhabi is a thriving, cosmopolitan city in the heart of the Middle East. The last few years have seen a staggering amount of development as the city has been transformed into a business hub and a tourist hotspot.

Explorer brings you insider knowledge of the sights and sounds of Abu Dhabi, from the traditional souks and the modern metropolis of the city to the rugged deserts beyond the UAE capital.

For more information about Abu Dhabi and the UAE, plus up-to-the-minute events and exciting new releases from Explorer, log onto **askexplorer.com**, where you can also give us your own take on this unique city.

There's more to life...
The Explorer Team

askexplorer.com

Contents

Essentials

Welcome To Abu Dhabi

From its origins as a centre for pearl diving and fishing, Abu Dhabi has developed at breakneck speed to become a truly 21st century destination.

As the capital of the United Arab Emirates, this is one of the world's most prosperous and rapidly developing cities. In little over half a century it has seen a dramatic transformation from a small Bedouin settlement to a thriving business and tourism centre of global stature.

The UAE sits on the north-eastern part of the Arabian Peninsula, bordered by Saudi Arabia to the south and west and by Oman to the east and north. The country is made up of seven emirates of which Abu Dhabi is by far the largest, occupying over 85% of the landmass. There are two major cities within the emirate: Abu Dhabi and Al Ain, which lies at the foot of the Hajar Mountains on the border with Oman.

The island city of Abu Dhabi is a lush, modern metropolis which has a lot to offer to visitors with its tree-lined streets, futuristic skyscrapers, huge shopping malls and international luxury hotels. The city is surrounded by the sparkling azure waters of the Arabian Gulf which present a striking contrast to the large parks and green boulevards that spread across the urban island.

Built on a grid system running from a central 'T', the city is easy to navigate. The 'T' is formed by the Corniche (p.90), which runs along the end of the island furthest from the mainland, and Airport Road which runs the length of the island. Roads running horizontally have odd numbers (the Corniche is 1st Street) and roads running vertically have even numbers (Airport Road is 2nd Street, with 4th Street, 6th Street, etc. leading off to the east, and 24th Street, 26th Street, etc. to the west).

With much of the interior of the emirate comprising desert, including part of the spectacular Rub Al Khali (Empty Quarter), or sabkha (salt flats), many visitors are surprised by how green the cities are. The combination of high temperatures and inhospitable terrain limits the variety of natural fauna and flora but the Abu Dhabi authorities are working hard to 'green' the urban landscape. Everywhere you look you'll see manicured lawns, pretty flowers and an abundance of palm trees which are maintained by an army of workers.

Over the next few pages you'll discover Abu Dhabi's rich cultural history, which should prove to be a good framework for your trip. There is plenty of advice about what to do when you first arrive and where to go when you are ready to explore. For tips on the must-do activities during your stay see p.22. The Exploring chapter (p.78) highlights the key areas and their cultural highlights including the museums and heritage sites. Sports & Spas (p.154) gives you the lowdown on some of the best activities in the emirate – from watersports to decadent spa treatments. The Shopping chapter (p.186) is a handy guide to the various souks and malls and includes tips on where to pick up those key buys (p.192). When it's time to fuel up, turn to the Going Out section (p.214) for the best restaurants, clubs and bars in the city and in Al Ain.

Culture & Heritage

The rich cultural legacy of this region runs alongside its innovative architecture, multicultural community and rapid growth.

Settling On Abu Dhabi Island

Despite the opportunities for fishing and grazing, it was not until the discovery of freshwater, in 1793, that the ruling Al Nahyan family, based in the south of the country at the Liwa Oasis, moved to Abu Dhabi island. In Liwa, on the edge of the stark Empty Quarter, the Al Nahyan family lived a traditional Bedouin life, with animal husbandry and small-scale agriculture for their livelihood. Descendants of the Al Nahyan family, in alliance with other important Bedouin tribes in the region, have ruled the emirate of Abu Dhabi ever since.

The Trucial States

By the 1800s, the town had developed considerably, supported by the income from pearling, which brought in important trade and revenue. From 1855 to 1909, under the reign of Sheikh Zayed bin Mohammed (also known as 'Zayed the Great'), Abu Dhabi rose in prominence to become the most powerful emirate along the western coast of the Arabian Peninsula. His influence was profound and it was during his rule, in 1897, that Abu Dhabi and the emirates to the north accepted the protection of Britain. The British regarded the Gulf region as an important communication

Traditional dhow

link with their empire in India and wanted to prevent other world powers, in particular France and Russia, from extending their influence in the region. The area became known as the Trucial States (or Trucial Coast), a name that remained until the United Arab Emirates was born in 1971.

Independence

The British announced their withdrawal from the region in 1968 and encouraged the separate states to consider uniting under one flag. The ruling sheikhs – in particular Sheikh Zayed bin Sultan Al Nahyan and the ruler of Dubai, His Highness Sheikh Rashid bin Saeed Al Maktoum – realised that by joining forces they would have a stronger voice in both the wider Middle East region and globally. When negotiations began, the aim was to create a single state consisting of Bahrain, Qatar and the Trucial States, but the process collapsed when Bahrain and Qatar chose to go it alone. The Trucial States remained committed to forming an alliance and, in 1971, the federation of the United Arab Emirates was created.

Formation Of The UAE

The new state comprised the emirates of Abu Dhabi, Ajman, Dubai, Fujairah, Sharjah, Umm Al Quwain and, by 1972, Ras Al Khaimah (each emirate is named after its main town). Under the agreement, the individual emirates each retained a certain degree of autonomy, with Abu Dhabi and Dubai providing the most input into the federation. The leaders of the new federation elected the ruler of Abu Dhabi, His Highness Sheikh Zayed bin Sultan Al Nahyan, to be their president, a position he held until he passed away on 2 November 2004. His eldest son, His Highness Sheikh Khalifa bin Zayed Al Nahyan, was then elected to take over the presidency.

The Discovery Of Oil

The formation of the UAE came after the discovery of huge oil reserves in Abu Dhabi in 1958. Abu Dhabi has an incredible 10% of the world's known oil reserves. Exports began four years later, launching Abu Dhabi on its way to incredible wealth.

Government & Ruling Family

The Supreme Council of Rulers is the highest authority in the UAE, comprising the hereditary rulers of the seven emirates. It is responsible for general policy involving education, defence, foreign affairs, communications and development, and for ratifying federal laws. Each emirate has one single vote, and the rulers of Abu Dhabi and Dubai have power of veto.

The Federal National Council (FNC) reports to the Supreme Council. It has executive authority to initiate and implement laws and is a

An Admired Ruler

Sheikh Zayed bin Sultan Al Nahyan was revered by his peers and adored by the public. As UAE president for 33 years and Ruler of Abu Dhabi from 1966 to 2004, he was responsible for many major economic and social advances both in Abu Dhabi and throughout the country, and his vision laid the foundations for today's modern society.

consultative assembly of 40 representatives, half of whom are chosen for the post in the FNC Elections. The individual emirates have some degree of autonomy, and laws that affect everyday life vary to some degree.

Culture

The UAE's culture is tolerant and welcoming, and visitors are sure to be charmed by the genuine friendliness of the people. Abu Dhabi is a melting pot of nationalities and cultures and the city's effort to become modern and cosmopolitan is proof of an open-minded and liberal outlook. There's a healthy balance between western influences and eastern traditions. For example, women face no discrimination and are able to drive and walk around the city unescorted, unlike in neighbouring Saudi Arabia.

The rapid economic development of the last 40 years has, in many ways, changed life in the UAE beyond recognition. However, despite rapid development and increased exposure to foreign influences, indigenous traditions and culture are alive and thriving. The people of Abu Dhabi enthusiastically promote cultural and sporting events that are representative of their past, such as falconry, camel racing and traditional dhow sailing. Arabic poetry, dances, songs and traditional art are encouraged, and weddings and celebrations are still colourful occasions with feasting and music. As a mark of pride in the culture and national identity, most locals wear traditional national dress. For men, this is a dishdash(a) or khandura – a full length shirt-dress that is worn with a white or red checked head-dress (gutra) which is held in place with

Al Ain Fort

a black cord (agal). Women wear a black abaya (a long, loose black robe) and a sheyla (a head scarf). Some women also wear a thin black veil to cover their faces and older women sometimes wear a leather mask (burkha).

Food & Drink

Traditional Arabic coffee (kahwa) is served on many occasions and, if offered, it is gracious to accept because coffee plays a special role as a symbolic expression of welcome. Even the pot itself, with its characteristic shape and long spout, has come to depict Arabic hospitality. Freshly ground and flavoured with cardamom, Arabic coffee comes in tiny cups with no handles. The cup should be taken with the right

hand. The server will stand by with the pot and fill the cups when empty. It's normal to accept one or two servings, then signal you have had enough by shaking the cup gently from side to side. Until you shake the cup, the server will continue topping it up.

Pork is not part of the Arabic menu and the consumption of it is taboo to a Muslim. Many restaurants don't serve it, though you should find it on the menu in some of the larger hotels and it is also available in some supermarkets.

Local Cuisine

Abu Dhabi's restaurant scene has a truly global flavour, with most of the world's major national cuisines represented, and many of the fast food outlets too. Eating out is very popular, but people tend to go out late so restaurants are often quiet in the early evenings. Modern Arabic cuisine reflects a blend of Moroccan, Tunisian, Iranian and Egyptian cooking styles, but the term usually refers to Lebanese food. From pavement stands serving mouth-watering shawarma (lamb or chicken sliced from a spit) and falafel (mashed and fried chickpea balls) sandwiches to the more elaborate khouzi (whole roast lamb served on a bed of rice, mixed with nuts), it's all here.

Religion

Islam, the official religion in the UAE, is widely practised. The religion is based on five pillars (Faith, Prayer, Charity, Fasting and Pilgrimage) and Muslims are called upon to pray five times a day, with these times varying according to the position of the sun. It is worth keeping in mind that Islam is more than just a religion; it is the basis for a complete way of life that all Muslims adhere to. There are plenty of mosques dotted around the city and, while most people pray in them when possible, most offices and public buildings have rooms set aside for prayers. Also, it's not unusual to see people kneeling by the side of the road if they are not near a mosque at prayer times. It is considered impolite to stare at people praying or to walk over prayer mats. The abundance of mosques means that the call to prayer can be heard five times a day from the loudspeakers of the many different minarets, and not always in sync. Friday is the Islamic holy day and pretty much everything is closed until mid-afternoon, in accordance with state and Islamic law.

During the holy month of Ramadan, Muslims are obliged to fast during daylight hours. Non-Muslims should not eat, drink or smoke in public areas during the fasting hours. You should also dress more conservatively. At sunset, the fast is broken with the Iftar feast. All over the city, festive Ramadan tents are filled each evening with people of all nationalities and religions enjoying shisha and traditional Arabic mezze and sweets. In addition to the shisha cafes and restaurants around town, many hotels erect special Ramadan tents.

The timing of Ramadan is not fixed in terms of the western calendar, but each year it occurs approximately 11 days earlier than the previous year, with the start date depending on the sighting of the moon. Parks and shops open and close later (many are closed during the day), entertainment such as live music is stopped, and cinemas limit daytime screenings. Eid Al Fitr (the feast of the breaking of the fast) is a three-day celebration and holiday at the end of Ramadan, when the new moon is spotted. It is the year's main religious event, like Diwali for Hindus and Christmas for Christians.

National Dress

On the whole, Emiratis wear their traditional dress in public. For men, this is the dishdash(a) or khandura – a white, full length shirt-dress which is worn with a white or red checked head-dress, known as a gutra. This is secured with a black cord (agal). Sheikhs and important businessmen may also wear a thin black or gold robe, or bisht, over their dishdasha at important events (equivalent to a dinner jacket).

In public, women wear the black abaya – a long, loose black robe that covers their normal clothes – plus a head scarf called the sheyla. They are often far from plain, with intricate embroidery and beadwork along the wrists and hemline; sheylas are also becoming more elaborate and a statement of individuality, particularly among the young.

The head wear varies with some women wearing a thin black veil covering their face and others, generally older women, wearing burkhas – a leather mask which covers the nose, brow and cheekbones. Underneath the abaya, the older women traditionally wear a long tunic over loose trousers (sirwall), often heavily embroidered and fitted at the wrists and ankles. Younger females are just as fashion conscious as in other countries and often wear designer labels with trendy accessories underneath their abayas.

Modern Abu Dhabi

The future of the emirate promises to be spectacular, with new developments bringing museums of international renown and luxury hotels.

Abu Dhabi has undergone tremendous growth over the past decade. Huge development projects are either on the way or have been finished. However, despite its immense wealth and impressive progress, Abu Dhabi did not remain completely untouched by the financial crisis of 2009; progress on some of the most significant projects in Abu Dhabi slowed, and other projects were scaled back a little as the UAE's GDP growth stalled.

Nevertheless, Abu Dhabi's oil wealth meant that the capital could afford to ride out the storm (and even extend Dubai a $10 billion loan to fight off its own creditors) to return to solid growth by 2010. Furthermore, that momentum has continued, thanks in part to Abu Dhabi's sizeable public investment spending and rising oil prices.

Boosting Abu Dhabi's infrastructure and manufacturing sector is central to the UAE's plans to wean its economy off oil. Tourism will play an ever larger part in any future growth, especially with the creation of Saadiyat Island's cultural district in full swing, while the government is making the emirate increasingly attractive to foreign investment with the establishment of Free Trade Zones and the formation of the impressive Central Business District on Al Maryah Island.

People & Economy

The UAE population has grown rapidly in recent years as expat arrivals, robust economic expansion and high birth rates have continued to push up the total number.

According to World Bank statistics, the UAE's population stood at 9.2 million by the end of 2012 with the capital's population estimated at 2.3 million. The UAE Statistics Bureau's figures show that the country's population has more than doubled (55% growth) since 2005, primarily due to a high number of other nationalities immigrating to the county.

The UAE is among the world's richest countries on a per capita basis. It is the second richest Arab country, after Qatar, thanks to its significant oil wealth. The country has just under 10% of the world's proven oil reserves (most of it within Abu Dhabi emirate) and the fourth largest natural gas reserves. At $284.4 billion, the UAE economy is the second largest in the Gulf, after Saudi Arabia. Successful economic diversification means that the UAE's wealth is no longer solely reliant on oil revenue; services alone account for more than half of the GDP. The International Monetary Fund (IMF) forecast the country's non-oil sector to grow 4.3% in mid 2013, up from 3.5% in the previous year.

The Abu Dhabi Economic Vision 2030 is a blueprint that aims to lead the emirate's economy into a highly diversified future, focused on acquisitions, aerospace, energy and industry, healthcare, infrastructure, real estate and hospitality, communications and service ventures. Sustainable growth as well as environmental sustainability will also continue to be a key criteria.

Tourism

Abu Dhabi was previously viewed by many as Dubai's lesser-known sibling but, in recent years, the capital has set itself up to become a major tourist destination in its own right. The city has recently witnessed an unprecedented boom in both plans for and construction of new hotels, amusement and theme parks, shopping malls, sports and recreational facilities, and art galleries and museums. Luxurious tourist resorts, including the Emirates Palace hotel (p.68), have put Abu Dhabi on the global tourism map. Outside the city, there's now a handful of classy resort hotels and attractions, such as Al Ain Zoo, being developed to widen the offering.

Meanwhile, significant investments are being made in the UAE's national carrier, Etihad Airways, to boost connections to the capital in the lead-up to completion of the tourist facilities. But it's not just leisure travel that the emirate is going for. The Abu Dhabi National Exhibition Centre, which opened in 2007, has contributed greatly to the number of business events held in town and Abu Dhabi is gearing up to become a major business tourism destination as well.

Abu Dhabi attracted around over 2.5 million visitors in the first 11 months of 2013, with over 260,000 visitors in November alone. The whole of the UAE attracted over 11 million visitors over the same period. Abu Dhabi is targeting 3.7 million visitors per year by 2017 and 7.2 million by 2030.

New Developments

When you see the amount of new development taking place in Abu Dhabi, it is easy to understand why the city is

Aldar headquarters

estimating three million yearly visitors by 2015. Billions of dirhams are being invested to transform the city into the cultural capital of the Arab world and many key projects focus on art, design and architecture. Added to this, the emirate is investing heavily to create outdoor facilities from beaches to golf courses and parks, and several new hotel resorts.

For those keen to hit the shops, Central Market, set just back from the Corniche, opened in early 2011 with the rest of the giant World Trade Center development opening its doors last year. The Saadiyat Island development, located just north of the city, will boost Abu Dhabi's cultural offerings. Already home to a number of beautiful beach hotels, the Monte-Carlo Beach Club, a golf course and the Manarat Al Saadiyat visitors' and exhibition centre – where interesting art

is regularly on display – the island will see the completion of the Sheikh Zayed National Museum, the Louvre Abu Dhabi, as well as the Guggenheim Abu Dhabi over the next few years. Saadiyat's neighbour, Yas Island, continues to hog plenty of the spotlight with Yas Waterworld now open and a giant mall soon to join the Yas hotels, Yas Marina Circuit (home to the Formula 1 grand prix), the Yas Marina complex and Ferrari World Abu Dhabi, the world's largest indoor theme park.

Abu Dhabi's flagship green project, Masdar City, is being developed near the airport. It will eventually be one of the world's most sustainable cities, powered entirely by renewable energy, and several parts of the city are already up-and-running. Find out more about the project at masdar.ae.

The Western Region of the Abu Dhabi emirate is officially known as Al Gharbia. This geographically stunning 60,000 square kilometre area contains not only some of the country's richest oil and gas reserves; it's also home to spectacular natural scenery, delicate ecosystems, traditional Bedouin culture and new tourism facilities. The redevelopment of the Desert Islands (desertislands.com) to create luxurious, sustainable eco-resorts is particularly worth checking out.

To cope with the rapid expansion, a state-of-the-art terminal is being constructed at Abu Dhabi International Airport. Eventually, the airport's passenger capacity will increase to 20-40 million per annum. Development includes a new runway, air traffic control tower, cargo and catering facilities. The national carrier, Etihad Airways, which began operations in 2003, has grown quickly. By the end of 2013, the airline was flying to 94 international destinations worldwide.

Abu Dhabi Checklist

01 Sheikh Zayed Grand Mosque

Sheikh Zayed Grand Mosque is one of the largest mosques in the world, and certainly one of the most beautiful. Walk around on your own, or take a complimentary tour to learn about Islamic worship.

02 Cruise The Corniche

The Corniche has undergone massive reconstruction and the scenic beach promenade is a popular spot for walks and strolls; alternatively, bikes can be rented for Dhs.20 for the day near the Hiltonia. For the best views that Abu Dhabi has to offer, a boat cruise along the Corniche (p.90) cannot be beaten.

03 Al Ain Oasis

This shaded, tranquil oasis contains many plantations, some of which are still working farms with ancient falaj irrigation systems. A peaceful and idyllic haven, the oasis is a great place for a stroll in the cooler months or to escape from the city.

04 Explore The Forts

Al Ain alone has 42 forts (more than any other Arabian city). Forts worth visiting in Al Ain include Al Jahili Fort & Park (p.130), Hili Fort in Buraimi (p.128), and the ancient Muraijib Fort (UAE Overview Map). In Abu Dhabi city, Al Maqtaa Fort (p.108) dates back 200 years.

05 Enjoy Desert Delights

Take an organised tour (p.150) to experience the vast Arabian desert in style and comfort. After a thrilling rollercoaster drive over the dunes, you'll enjoy a sumptuous barbecue under the stars at a Bedouin camp, complete with henna painting, camel riding and the sultry moves of a belly dancer.

06 Relax On A Desert Island

Located 250km from Abu Dhabi city, the desert islands are worth the long journey to enjoy the exclusive Desert Islands resort and get up close to nature at the Arabian Wildlife Park on Sir Bani Yas Island. The Al Gharbia Region is a definite up-and-comer on Abu Dhabi's tourism roll-call.

07 Indulge In Luxury

There's no shortage of luxurious hotels in Abu Dhabi, but the iconic Emirates Palace (p.68) is the cream of the crop; even if you're not staying in one of the 392 opulent rooms and suites, a visit here is a must. Book an afternoon tea and arrive early to take in the sheer size and splendour of the landmark hotel.

08 Charter A Dhow

Before the discovery of oil most islanders made their living from the sea, either fishing or pearl diving. Nowadays, dhows are a fantastic way to explore the islands (p.120), offering a new perspective on their stunning scenery and abundant marine wildlife (see Dhow Charters, p.158).

09 Shop 'Til You Drop

Whether you're looking for designer labels or just souvenirs, the many malls (p.200) and souks (p.196) are packed with ways to part with your hard-earned cash. Abu Dhabi Gold Souk, located in Madinat Zayed, is home to some of the largest gold shops in the Gulf, and the range of jewellery available is staggering.

10 Try Life In The Fast Lane

Explore Yas Island (p.122), home to Yas Marina Circuit (p.170) which hosts the annual Abu Dhabi grand prix (p.58), the spectacular Yas Viceroy (p.72), Ferrari World Abu Dhabi (p.170) and Yas Waterworld (p.168). Yas Marina, Yas Links and Yas Beach make it a must-visit, even before the giant Yas Mall arrives in 2014.

11 Discover Liwa

Liwa is a destination that will blow you away with its massive expanses of untouched desert and the biggest sand dunes this side of the Sahara. The drive down there is long, but it's a once-in-a-lifetime opportunity to experience unforgettable sunrises and adventurous off-road driving.

12 The Heritage Village

The Heritage Village (p.86) offers a glimpse into a way of life and culture that is far removed from the cosmopolitan and globalised city we see today. Test the effectiveness of a wind tower, the earliest form of air conditioning, make friends with a camel, or brush up on traditional arts and crafts.

Best Of Abu Dhabi

For Adrenaline Junkies

The UAE has a lot to offer outdoor enthusiasts. There's a good range of terrain for mountain bikers, from super-technical rocky trails in areas like Shuwayah and Shawka, to mountain routes like Jebel Yibir which climb to over a thousand metres and can be descended in minutes. Dubai-based club Hot Cog MTB (hot-cog.com) is an active group that welcomes new members. Dune and wadi bashing are popular pastimes in the UAE. The desert, mountains and wadis offer stunning scenery and great challenges for experienced and novice drivers alike. Various tour companies run courses where you can learn the art of manoeuvring a 4WD over dunes. For several adventures all within the one complex, head for Wadi Adventure (p.131), where surfing, rapids, climbing and zip lines await.

For Big Spenders

There is no shortage of places to shop in Abu Dhabi, whether you are after the international brands and designer stores in the malls or a more authentic Arabian experience in the souks. Abu Dhabi Mall (p.200) is one of the biggest of the bunch, while Bawabat Al Sharq Mall and Dalma Mall are two of the most recent additions; Central Market and Souk Qaryat Al Beri, on the other hand, provide atmospheric options. Local produce and traditional items can also be picked up at the souks. They are worth a visit for their bustling atmosphere, variety of goods, and the traditional way of doing business. If you still have a shopping itch take the short trip over to Dubai to experience The Dubai Mall (thedubaimall.com), which is likely to challenge the most experienced shopaholic.

Sheikh Zayed Grand Mosque

For Culture Buffs

The great cultural attraction in Abu Dhabi is the big, beautiful Sheikh Zayed Bin Sultan Al Nahyan Mosque, commonly known as the Grand Mosque (see p.108). The Abu Dhabi Tourism & Culture Authority (tcaabudhabi.ae) has a location near Zayed Sports City which is home to the National Archives and the National Library. The foundation is a hive of activity with art classes, pottery and language classes regularly held. If your visit to the region has given you a taste for local art, visit the Women's Handicraft Centre (p.141) just off Airport Road. Here you'll see women practising traditional arts (textile weaving, embroidering, basket weaving, palm frond weaving and tailoring); you can also pick up a camel bag and all manner of traditional craft items.

For Foodies

Arabic treats are a must while you are in town, whether you try one of the lively eateries such as Mawal (p.261) at The Hilton Abu Dhabi or Li Beirut (p.260) at Jumeirah at Etihad Towers, or opt for streetside stands selling shawarma (rolled pita bread filled with lamb or chicken) and salad.

For Water Babies

There is plenty of fun to be had in the water, from diving to wakeboarding and waterskiing at the various beach clubs; the Hiltonia (p.181) is a perennial favourite while those preferring a more relaxed but opulent experience might like to head for the Monte-Carlo Beach Club, Saadiyat (p.182). The new Yas Waterworld (p.168) brings some much-needed water park fun to Abu Dhabi.

For Architecture Admirers

The dramatic evolution of Abu Dhabi into a modern day metropolis brings a wealth of innovative architecture. The spectacular Ferrari World, the majestic Capital Gate (capitalgate.ae), Sowwah Square on Al Maryah and the circular Aldar HQ building near Al Raha are all design gems.

For Party People

Sip cocktails and show off your best moves at Cinnabar (02 681 1900), Etoiles at Emirates Palace(02 690 8960) or Skylite Lounge and Rush at the Yas Viceroy (p.72). O1NE Yas Island (052 788 8111) is a dedicated nightclub for the clubbing elite on Yas Island, open every Thursday only.

Monte-Carlo Beach Club, Saadiyat

Visiting Abu Dhabi

The UAE warmly welcomes visitors and you can expect nothing less than exemplary hospitality, a growing infrastructure, and plenty to see.

Getting There

Abu Dhabi International Airport is undergoing a major expansion and redevelopment programme (see p.18). Terminal 3, exclusively for Etihad flights, opened in 2009 and more additions are on the way. The aircraft gates at the other terminals are arranged around a circular satellite, so you won't have to walk far to reach immigration and the baggage reclaim area. If you haven't arranged a hotel limousine pick up or hire car, a taxi to the city centre will cost about Dhs.65.

Completion of Abu Dhabi International Airport expansion is also expected to contribute to the boom in tourism. The project will upgrade the capacity of the airport to 20-40 million passengers a year. More than 40 airlines now operate out of the international airport with the key player being the UAE's national airline, Etihad Airways.

The airline first launched flights in 2003, greatly increasing the accessibility of the city to international travellers. Etihad flies to six continents and has been adding new routes on a near weekly basis of late, so chances are you'll find flights to and from your destination. Dubai-bound passengers get to benefit from free coach transfers between Abu Dhabi and Dubai.

Airport Transfer

There is a regular bus service between Abu Dhabi International Airport and the city centre. The fully air-conditioned, green and white A1 bus runs every 40 minutes, 24 hours a day, from outside the arrivals halls of Terminals 1 and 3. The fare is Dhs.4, however you will need to purchase an Ojra card (ojra.ae) or have the exact change. Bus route maps are available from the airport (02 505 5555) or online.

Airlines

Air France	800 23823	airfrance.ae
Alitalia	02 622 2888	alitalia.com
Austrian Airlines	02 677 6621	austrian.com
British Airways	02 611 8600	britishairways.com
Cathay Pacific	02 617 6000	cathaypacific.com
Delta Airlines	02 671 3033	delta.com
Egypt Air	02 634 4777	egyptair.com
Emirates Airline	600 555 555	emirates.com
Etihad Airways	02 511 0000	etihadairways.com
flydubai	04 231 1000	flydubai.com
Gulf Air	02 651 6888	gulfair.com
Jazeera Airways	02 224 4464	jazeeraairways.com
KLM Royal Dutch Airways	800 23823	klm.com
Kuwait Airways	02 631 2230	kuwait-airways.com
Lufthansa	02 639 4640	lufthansa.com
Middle East Airlines	02 622 6300	mea.com.lb
Qatar Airways	02 621 0007	qatarairways.com

Visas & Customs

Visa requirements for entering Abu Dhabi vary greatly between different nationalities, and regulations should always be checked before travelling, since details can change with little or no warning. GCC nationals (Bahrain, Kuwait, Qatar, Oman and Saudi Arabia) do not need a visa to enter Abu Dhabi. Citizens from many other countries (see Visas On Arrival, p.41) get an automatic visa upon arrival at the airport. The entry visa is valid for 30 days, although you can renew for a further 30 days at a cost of Dhs.500. Other nationalities can get a 30 day tourist visa sponsored by a local entity, such as a hotel or tour operator, before entry. The fee is Dhs.110, and the visa can be renewed for a further 30 days for Dhs.500. Some airlines can also apply for your visa, or if you have a family member resident in the UAE then they can apply for you, so long as they meet certain criteria.

A special transit visa (up to 14 days) may be obtained through certain airlines operating in the UAE for a small fee, although Europeans can just get the free 30 day visit visa. Citizens from Somalia, Afghanistan, Iraq, Nigeria and Yemen are not currently accepted for a transit visa, but check with your carrier before booking.

Certain medications, including codeine, Temazepam and Prozac, are banned even though they are freely available in other countries. There have been some high-profile cases that have highlighted the UAE's zero tolerance to drugs. Even a miniscule quantity in your possession could result in a lengthy jail term. Bags will be scanned to ensure you have no offending magazines or DVDs too.

Visa On Arrival

Citizens of the following countries receive an automatic visa on arrival in Abu Dhabi: Andorra, Australia, Austria, Belgium, Brunei, Canada, Denmark, Finland, France, Germany, Greece, Hong Kong, Iceland, Ireland, Italy, Japan, Liechtenstein, Luxembourg, Malaysia, Monaco, Netherlands, New Zealand, Norway, Portugal, San Marino, Singapore, South Korea, Spain, Sweden, Switzerland, United Kingdom, United States of America and Vatican City.

Dos & Don'ts

The UAE is one of the most tolerant and liberal states in the Gulf region. As a visitor, there still isn't much that you can't do or wear: just a healthy amount of respect for local customs will do, especially when shopping or sightseeing. Women should be aware that revealing clothing can attract unwanted attention, so very short skirts and strapless tops should be avoided. It is especially recommended that you dress more conservatively during Ramadan. Like most places in the world, the rural areas have a more conservative attitude than in the cities. Lewd and drunken behaviour is not only disrespectful but can lead to arrest and detention. There is also zero tolerance to drinking and driving. Abu Dhabi is full of snap-worthy sights and normal tourist photography is fine. However, it is courteous to ask permission before photographing people, particularly women. With prices for cigarettes low, smoking is very common, but new laws have banned lighting up in malls and some restaurants so it's best to check the policy.

Local Knowledge

Abu Dhabi is an open-minded and hospitable emirate, where visitors from all over the world are made to feel both welcome and safe.

Climate

Abu Dhabi has a sub-tropical, arid climate and sunny blue skies and high temperatures can be expected most of the year. Rainfall is sporadic, falling mainly in winter (November to March). Rainfall averages 12cm per year in most of the emirate, but rain is more common in Al Ain due to its proximity to the Hajar mountains. Temperatures range from a low of around 12°C (54°F), on a winter's night, to a high of around 42°C (118°F), on a summer's day. The cooler months, November to April, are the most pleasant time to visit, when temperatures are around 24°C (75°F) during the day and 13°C (56°F) at night.

There are occasional sandstorms, when the wind whips the sand off the desert. This is not to be confused with a shamal, a north-westerly wind that comes off the Arabian Gulf and can cool temperatures down. Sandstorms cover everything left outside in gardens or balconies and can even blow inside, so make sure your windows and doors are shut fast.

Thick fog occasionally sets in on winter mornings, but is invariably burnt off by mid morning. The humidity can be a killer in the summer, making it feel far hotter than it actually is in July, August and September.

Crime & Safety

While the crime rate in Abu Dhabi is very low, a healthy degree of caution should still be exercised. It is unlikely that you will be the victim of a scam or a robbery, but it still pays to keep your wits about you. Keep your valuables and travel documents locked in your hotel safe and when in crowds, be discreet with your money and don't carry large amounts of cash on you. Don't use an ATM if it looks like it may have been tampered with and inform your bank.

If you are crossing the road on foot, use designated pedestrian crossings (jaywalking is illegal), and make sure the cars are really going to stop before crossing. If you plan on driving yourself, make sure you know the rules of the road, exercise extreme caution, pay attention to your mirrors, and be aware of what's happening around you at all times.

Useful Numbers

Abu Dhabi Municipality	800 22 220
Emergency	999
Abu Dhabi International Airport	02 505 5555
Al Ain International Airport	02 505 5000
Taxi	600 53 5353
UAE Country Code	00 971
Abu Dhabi Area Code	02
Al Ain Area Code	03
Directory Enquiries (du)	199
Directory Enquiries (Etisalat)	181

Police

Abu Dhabi has a large, active, and highly respected police force. The uniforms are easily identifiable: the standard uniform is ash-grey but traffic police wear white sleeves and a white belt to differentiate themselves. Police vehicles are generally red and white with blue and red lights on the roof. The police are very approachable, and they will respond promptly if there is a problem.

In An Emergency

Abu Dhabi is among the safest and most crime-free places in the world. Despite this, accidents and bad things do happen. The emergency telephone number is 999 and you can use it if you are involved in a traffic accident or to report a crime. If any valuables go missing, check with your hotel first; or if you've lost something in a taxi, call the firm's lost and found department. There are a lot of honest people in Abu Dhabi who will return found items. If you've had no luck, then call Abu Dhabi Police to report the loss or theft; you'll be advised on the next steps to follow. Also, keep a passport photocopy in a secure place to avoid hassle should you misplace it.

Electricity & Water

Electricity and water services in Abu Dhabi are excellent and power cuts or water shortages are practically unheard of. The electricity supply is 220/240 volts and 50 cycles. Sockets are mostly three pin of the British style, but some are two pin. The tap water is heavily purified and safe to drink, but most people prefer to drink locally bottled mineral water for the taste.

Female Visitors

Women should face few, if any, problems while travelling in the UAE. Women who are alone and who don't want extra attention should avoid wearing tight or revealing clothing and should steer clear of lower-end hotels and seedy nightclubs. No matter what, most women receive some unwanted stares at some time or another, particularly on the public beaches (periodically there is a crackdown on anyone suspected of harassing or staring at women on the beach). If you find yourself unable to escape an unwanted conversation, the mention of a husband (even a fictional one) should help you make a polite but firm getaway. The police are helpful and respectful – call them at any time if you face any unwanted attention.

It is perfectly acceptable to wear summery tops, skirts and shorts, especially in the more 'expat' areas. If you venture into more traditional or Arabic areas, it is best to dress modestly. In other parts of the country with less of an expat community, it's advisable to dress as respectfully as the weather allows.

Money

Most large shops, hotels and restaurants accept the major credit cards. Some credit card companies still like to know of your travel plans before you leave your home country; otherwise they might freeze your account if they suspect fraud. Smaller retailers are sometimes less keen to accept credit cards and you may have to pay an extra 5% for processing. Conversely, paying in cash might mean a discount, so don't be afraid to use this as a bargaining chip.

Cash is always your best option in the souks, unless buying expensive jewellery.

Money exchanges are available all over Abu Dhabi, they offer good service and reasonable exchange rates and are often better than the banks. Many hotels will also exchange money and travellers' cheques at the standard (poor) hotel rate. Be aware that exchanges tend to close between 13:00 and 16:30.

The monetary unit is the dirham (Dhs.) which is divided into 100 fils. Coin denominations are Dhs.1, 50 fils, 25 fils, 10 fils and 5 fils (although the latter two are very rare). Notes come in Dhs.5, 10, 20, 50, 100, 200, 500 and 1,000. The dirham has been tied to the US dollar since 1980 at a mid rate of $1 to Dhs.3.6725.

There is a huge network of local and international banks, strictly controlled by the UAE Central Bank. Hours are Saturday to Wednesday, 08:00 to 13:00 (some open 16:30 to 18:30) and Thursday, 08:00 to12:00. Branches located in the city centre may have longer opening hours.

All banks operate ATMs accepting a range of cards. For non-UAE based cards, the exchange rates used in the transaction are normally competitive and the process is faster than using travellers' cheques. ATMs can be found in the airport, shopping malls and most hotels, as well as petrol stations.

Language

Arabic is the official national language, although English, Hindi, Malayalam and Urdu are widely spoken. Arabic is the official business language, but English is widely used and

City nightscape

most road signs, shop signs and restaurant menus are in both languages. The further out of town you go, the more Arabic you will find, both written and spoken, on street and shop signs. See the table below for a quick list of useful Arabic phrases. Arabic isn't the easiest language to pick up, or to pronounce, but if you can throw in a couple of words of Arabic here and there, they will usually be warmly received. Most people will help you out with your pronunciation.

Basic Arabic

General

Yes	na'am
No	la
Please	min fadlak (m)/min fadliki (f)
Thank you	shukran
Praise be to God	al-hamdu l-illah
God willing	in shaa'a l-laah

Greetings

Greeting (peace be upon you)	as-salaamu alaykom
Greeting (in reply)	wa alaykom is salaam
Good morning	sabah il-khayr
Good morning (in reply)	sabah in-nuwr
Good evening	masa il-khayr
Good evening (in reply)	masa in-nuwr
Hello	marhaba
Hello (in reply)	marhabtayn
How are you?	kayf haalak (m)/kayf haalik (f)
Fine, thank you	zayn, shukran (m)/zayna, shukran (f)

Welcome	ahlan wa sahlan
Goodbye	ma is-salaama
Introduction	
My name is...	ismiy…
What is your name?	shuw ismak? (m) / shuw ismik? (f)
Where are you from?	min wayn inta (m) / min wayn (f)
Questions	
How many / much?	kam?
Where?	wayn?
When?	mataa?
Which?	ayy?
How?	kayf?
What?	shuw?
Why?	laysh?
And	wa
Numbers	
Zero	sifr
One	waahad
Two	ithnayn
Three	thalatha
Four	arba'a
Five	khamsa
Six	sitta
Seven	saba'a
Eight	thamaanya
Nine	tiss'a
Ten	ashara

People With Disabilities

Most of Abu Dhabi's five-star hotels have wheelchair facilities but, in general, facilities for people with disabilities are limited, particularly at tourist attractions. Wheelchair ramps are often really nothing more than delivery ramps, hence the steep angles. When asking if a location has wheelchair access, make sure it really does – an escalator is considered wheelchair access to some. The Abu Dhabi International Airport is well equipped for physically challenged travellers and it is easily accessible. There is a special check-in gate with direct access from the car park, as well as dedicated lifts, and a meet and assist service. Hotels with wheelchair accessible rooms include the following: Eastern Mangroves by Anantara, Emirates Palace, Le Royal Meridien Abu Dhabi, Crowne Plaza, Crowne Plaza Yas Island, Hilton Abu Dhabi, Millennium Hotel, InterContinental Abu Dhabi, Shangri-La Hotel Qaryat Al Beri, Westin Abu Dhabi Golf Resort & Spa, and the Danat Al Ain Resort.

Telephone & Internet

Etisalat and du are the local mobile telecoms companies and have reciprocal agreements with most countries for roaming services, allowing visitors to use their mobile in the UAE. Etisalat and du also offer useful prepaid services aimed at tourists. Visitors can purchase a SIM card and local number pre-loaded with calling credit so you can make local calls at the local rate. Both Etisalat and du SIM cards are available at most malls and mobile phone shops. Both of the local mobile telecoms offer short-term mobile lines for tourists. The lines can be picked up from one of the many Etisalat or du kiosks scattered throughout the big malls. The package includes a SIM card and usually a few minutes of calling credit that can be used for international calls or SMS. International calls from local mobile lines are much cheaper than hotel rates and you can buy extra credit at most supermarkets, newsstands and gas stations.

Time

Local time in Abu Dhabi is four hours ahead of UTC (Universal Coordinated Time, formerly GMT) with no summer saving time and so no clock changes. Thanks to the diversity of Abu Dhabi's residents and visitors, evenings are busy early on with families and late into the night with party-goers.

Tipping

It is entirely up to the individual whether to tip for services and it is not a fixed expectation as you may find in other countries. Service and luxury taxes are charged in hotel restaurants (which can add between 10% and 16% to the final bill). For those who feel that the service was worth recognising, the usual amount is 10% and tips are greatly appreciated. An increasing number of restaurants now also include a service charge on the bill, although it's not clear whether this ever sees the inside of your waiter's pockets, so some people add a little extra. For taxi drivers, it is regular practice to round up your fare as a tip, but this is not compulsory, so feel free to pay just the fare if the driving was below standard. For valet-parking tipping at hotels or malls, around Dhs.5 is the average.

Media & Further Reading

Newspapers & Magazines

The UAE has a number of daily English language broadsheets. The cream of the crop is definitely Abu Dhabi's The National, arguably the region's first national newspaper offering quality journalism, intelligent editorial and meaty lifestyle pieces. The National costs Dhs.3 and there's also a good online version at thenational.ae. Other newspapers include the Gulf News, the Khaleej Times and Gulf Today, all of which cover local, regional and international news and lifestyle issues. Additionally, many supermarkets carry a selection of international newspapers. In most areas of Abu Dhabi, you can also pick up a free copy of 7Days, a tabloid-size newspaper published five days a week that features local and international news, business and entertainment news, and a sports section.

Many of the major glossy magazines are available in Abu Dhabi, but if they're imported from the US or Europe, you can expect to pay at least twice the normal cover price. Alternatively, you can pick up the Middle East versions of popular titles including Harper's Bazaar, Grazia, OK! and Hello! where you'll find all the regular gossip and news, with extras from around the region.

All international titles are examined and, if necessary, censored to ensure that they don't offend the country's moral values.

Television

Most hotel rooms will have satellite or cable, broadcasting a decent mix of local and international channels. In terms of English channels, you'll find the major news stations and some BBC programming, in addition to the standard hotel room information loop.

The local television channels in Abu Dhabi are rapidly improving and they often show episodes of US talk shows and American sitcoms in addition to the local news programmes and Arabic sitcoms.

Radio

The UAE has a number of commercial radio stations broadcasting in a range of languages, including Arabic, English, French, Hindi, Malayalam and Urdu. The daily schedules are listed in all local newspapers.

The leading English language stations operate 24 hours a day and, while most are physically based in Dubai, they can usually be picked up with good reception throughout Abu Dhabi: Radio 1 (100.5FM & 104.1FM) and 2 (99.3FM & 106FM), Dubai 92 (92.0FM), Channel 4 (104.8FM), Virgin Radio (104.4FM) and The Coast (103.2FM).

More Info?

If you want to find out more about what's going on in Abu Dhabi, check out *askexplorer.com* for event listings. To venture out of the city, pick up a copy of *Short Breaks From & Within The UAE* for the low-down on the region's best hotels. The UAE *Off-Road Explorer* is essential reading if you want to explore the country, as is the *Ultimate UAE & Oman Explorer.*

Public Holidays

The Islamic calendar starts from the year 622AD, the year of Prophet Muhammad's migration (Hijra) from Mecca to Al Madinah. Hence the Islamic year is called the Hijri year and dates are followed by AH (After Hijra). As some holidays are based on the sighting of the moon and are not fixed dates on the Hijri calendar, the dates of Islamic holidays are more often than not confirmed less than 24 hours in advance. Some non-religious holidays, however, are fixed according to the Gregorian calendar.

The main Muslim festivals are Eid Al Fitr (the festival of the breaking of the fast, which marks the end of Ramadan) and Eid Al Adha (the festival of the sacrifice, which marks the end of the pilgrimage to Mecca). Mawlid Al Nabee is the holiday celebrating the Prophet Muhammad's birthday, and Lailat Al Mi'raj celebrates the Prophet's ascension into heaven.

In general, public holidays are unlikely to disrupt a visit to Abu Dhabi except that shops may open a bit later.

Public Holidays

New Year (1)	1 Jan 2014 (Fixed)
Mawlid Al Nabee	13 Jan 2014 (Moon)
Lailat Al Mi'raj (1)	26 May 2014 (Moon)
Eid Al Fitr (3)	28 July 2014 (Moon)
Arafat Day (1)	3 Oct 2014 (Moon)
Eid Al Adha (3)	4 Oct 2014 (Moon)
Islamic New Year's Day (1)	25 Oct 2014 (Moon)
UAE National Day (2)	2 Dec 2014 (Fixed)

During Ramadan, however, food and beverages cannot be consumed in public during daylight hours, while smoking is also prohibited. These rules apply to Muslims and non-Muslims alike. Women should also dress more conservatively during this time. Food outlets and restaurants generally remain closed or offer takeaway purchases only during the day and then open up for Iftar, the breaking of the fast, in the evening.

Annual Events

Throughout the year, the UAE hosts a number of major annual events which attract visitors from far and wide. The events listed below are some of the more popular fixtures on the social calendar. For up to the minute information on all events, check askexplorer.com.

Dhow Racing
All year round

Nr Marina Mall, Breakwater
adimsc.ae

Scheduled dhow races take place throughout the year, mostly between October and April. The ones held off Abu Dhabi are short coastal races and the boats, many of which are old pearling vessels, have a shallow draught ideal for sailing closer to the Corniche.

Abu Dhabi HSBC Golf Championship
January

Abu Dhabi Golf Club
Madinat Khalifa
abudhabigolfchampionship.com

With over $2 million in prize money up for grabs, and some of the biggest names in world golf appearing on the green, the

Abu Dhabi Golf Championship is one of the biggest sporting events in the capital each year.

Abu Dhabi Festival
March-April

Emirates Palace, Al Ras Al Akhdar — abudhabifestival.ae

Organised by the Abu Dhabi Music & Arts Foundation (ADMAF), this successful festival has brought big names in classical music and fine arts to the capital every year since 2004. In the past, the event has featured the likes of the Bolshoi Ballet, Andrea Bocelli, Sir James Galway and Yo-Yo Ma, among others.

Abu Dhabi Desert Challenge
April

Empty Quarter, Liwa — abudhabidesertchallenge.com

After the Abu Dhabi grand prix, this is the highest profile motorsport event in the country and is often the culmination of the cross-country rallying world cup. The event attracts some of the world's top rally drivers and bike riders who compete in the car, truck and motocross categories over four days. There are numerous checkpoints where the public can hang out to watch the daredevil participants scream past in their vehicles.

Al Gharbia Watersports Festival
April

Mirfa Public Beach, Al Gharbia — algharbiafestivals.com

From kiteboards and surf ski kayaks among the waves to chilled-out camping and concerts on shore, the 10 day watersports extravaganza has it all for the UAE's beach lovers. The event takes place on Mirfa's public beach and features world-class athletes, water fun, and beach activities from sandcastle building to volleyball.

Abu Dhabi Film Festival

October

Various locations — abudhabifilmfestival.ae

This festival has gone from strength to strength to become one of the region's premier film events. The past few years have seen stellar line-ups and, with more films, grants and awards, and more film stars and celebrities making appearances, the future looks promising. Uma Thurman, Clive Owen, Forest Whitaker, Tilda Swinton and Richard Gere have attended previous editions. In 2013. more Emirati films than ever were screened, highlighting its impact in the region.

Abu Dhabi Art

November

Manarat Al Saadiyat — abudhabiartfair.ae

Galleries and artists from across the region and the world come to exhibit work and take part in lectures, debates and workshops during this four day event. The airy spaces at Manarat Al Saadiyat and exhibition space in the UAE Pavilion on Saadiyat Island add an extra special reason to indulge in some artistic appreciation.

Al Ain Aerobatic Show

November-December

Al Ain International Airport, Al Ain — alainaerobaticshow.com

The Al Ain Air Show is a popular five-day event held at the airport just outside the oasis city. The show features flying daredevils from around the world performing aerobatic stunts and displays that truly wow the crowds.

Formula 1 Etihad Airways Abu Dhabi Grand Prix
November
Yas Marina Circuit, Yas Island
formula1.com

Racing fans and non-F1 devotees delight in this big weekend in November. As it is one of the last races of the F1 season, excitement is guaranteed on the track, while the event also features a number of big name entertainers performing on stage at the end of each day. Spectators can watch the F1 action from the grandstand or various seating sections around the track, while restaurant terraces at The Yas Viceroy are another option worth looking into.

Mubadala World Tennis Championship
December
Zayed Sports City, Al Madina Al Riyadiya
mubadalawtc.com

After a few years of hosting the world's top male players (Federer, Nadal, Murray, Djokovic) and attracting record crowds of up to 15,000 fans, this tournament has quickly become the hottest end of year sporting ticket in town. In addition to the matches themselves, a series of tennis-based activities and tournaments take place in the run-up to the event, including the Community Cup.

Powerboat Racing
December
Nr Marina Mall, Breakwater
adimsc.ae

The UAE is well established on the world championship powerboat racing circuit with Formula 1 (onshore) in Abu Dhabi and Class One (offshore) in Dubai and Fujairah. Abu Dhabi International Marine Sports Club hosts races from October to May, including the final round of the season.

Clockwise from top: camel racing, Formula 1 Etihad Airways Abu Dhabi Grand Prix, Al Gharbia Watersports Festival

ETIHAD
UBS

Getting Around

Abu Dhabi is compact, well laid out and easy to navigate. While public transportation is limited, there are more than enough alternatives.

A car (or taxi) is the most popular and practical method for getting around Abu Dhabi. There is a reasonable public bus service, which is a cost-effective mode of transport, and walking and cycling are an option during the cooler months, but as yet, there are no trains or trams.

Abu Dhabi's road network is excellent, and most main roads have at least three lanes. Streets are generally well-signposted with bilingual blue or green signs indicating the main areas or roads in and out of the city. There is an official street name and numbering system, with a new system being rolled out in 2014, but people often refer to streets by their colloquial name or rely on landmarks to give directions. The city's roads are built on a New York-style grid system and the Airport Road (2nd Street), which runs from the Corniche to Al Maqtaa Bridge, bisects the island. Abu Dhabi city used to be linked to the mainland by just two bridges, Al Maqtaa Bridge and Mussafah Bridge, but two more bridges have now opened: the Sheikh Zayed Bridge and Saadiyat Bridge.

Al Ain has developed in a less-organised manner, but is nevertheless based on a rough grid system. The city is fairly spread out, consisting of about 10 major roads. Roundabouts are important landmarks for giving directions.

Bus

Public transportation has improved a lot over the past few years. Bus routes now carry passengers all over the emirate, as well as the city. The service runs more or less around the clock and fares are inexpensive (as little as Dhs.2 for travel within the capital). The main bus station is on Hazza bin Zayed Road and there are bus stops in most residential districts. An increasing number of new bus shelters have been erected, some of which are air-conditioned.

'Ojra' bus passes can be purchased at the central bus station or at any Red Crescent kiosk. An unlimited use monthly pass costs Dhs.80. For more information, visit ojra.ae where full bus route maps can be found and downloaded. Those without passes can simply deposit Dhs.2 in the silver box upon entering the inter-urban bus. Later this year Hafilat rechargable payment cards that you swipe on entry and exit of the bus will replace the Ojra system. Buses are gender-segregated with a special ladies' section in the front.

The Abu Dhabi-Dubai Emirates Express is operated jointly by the Abu Dhabi and Dubai municipalities. The 150km route along Sheikh Zayed Road takes around two hours and operates reliably every 30 minutes between 06:30 and 21:30 at the central bus station in Abu Dhabi. Return buses leave Dubai's Al Ghubaibah station from 06:20 until 23:40. The cost per person has recently increased to Dhs.20 for a one- way ticket. There's an on-bus catering service available, and RTA introduced onboard Wi-Fi in 2012. Bus routes to the Western Region are also available at similarly inexpensive fares, if you don't mind spending a bit more time getting there than you would by car.

An express service (the X90) was recently introduced between Abu Dhabi and Al Ain, leaving every 30 minutes between 04:30 and 00:00 with a single stop in Khatem. One-way tickets cost Dhs.15 and the journey takes 90 minutes.

Driving & Car Hire

Abu Dhabi has built an impressive network of roads and construction continues as new areas are being developed; as a consequence, be prepared to come across lots of roadworks. While the infrastructure is superb, you should be aware that the standard of driving varies because there are drivers from all over the world behind the wheel here. As in any multicultural city, this means that you should be prepared for differences in driving styles. Overall, road safety has improved greatly thanks to the introduction of speed cameras and stricter traffic enforcement. Nonetheless, it's

Car Rental Agencies

Avis	Abu Dhabi Al Ain	02 575 7180 03 768 7262
Budget Rent A Car		02 443 8430
Diamondlease		02 674 0350
Euroline		052 999 555
Europcar	Abu Dhabi Al Ain	02 626 1441 03 721 0180
Hertz		02 672 0060
Thrifty	Abu Dhabi Al Ain	02 634 5663 03 721 8088

essential to stay alert and pay close attention to the traffic, and always use your mirrors and indicators. Driving is on the right hand side, wearing seat belts is mandatory in the front seats, and speed limits are usually around 60 to 80kph in town, and 100 to 120kph on major roads. These are increasingly strictly enforced by cameras.

You will find all the major car rental companies in Abu Dhabi, plus a few local ones. It is best to shop around as rates can vary considerably. The larger, more reputable firms generally have more reliable vehicles and a greater capacity to help in an emergency.

Taxi

Taxis are reasonably priced, plentiful and the most common method of getting around. The city has a 7,000 strong taxi fleet that is overseen by TransAD (transad.ae).

TransAD imposes stringent rules on drivers, regularly fining those who commit offences such as demanding a fare higher than that on the meter, or even refusing to stop when hailed (all Dhs.500 fines). Some drivers will try to negotiate their fare with you; keep in mind that this is illegal and you can insist on the meter. Taxi drivers' English skills vary and, infuriatingly, they are often not familiar with street names or places. It helps to know where you are going – take the phone number of your destination and a pocket map (such as Explorer's *Abu Dhabi Mini Map*) in case you get lost.

Taxis can either be flagged down at the roadside or booked by phone; you should have no trouble getting one from a mall or your hotel. All taxi companies service the airport but expect to ride in one of the new black cabs from the airport. These carry up to seven people, but have a flagfall of Dhs.25, rather than the usual Dhs.3.5 (although fares are the same). Budget around Dhs.80 for to get to the city.

Those with silver livery and a yellow sign on the roof are the regular taxis. Daytime (06:00-22:00) metered fares in the city start at Dhs.3.5 and increase by Dhs.1.6 for every subsequent kilometre of a journey. Most trips around the city shouldn't cost more than Dhs.15. Nighttime fares are slightly more, with the starting fare at Dhs.4 and a minimal fare of Dhs.10 after 22:00. The fare chart must be in plain view inside the taxi and, while tips are welcome, it's illegal for a driver to demand one. If you have any problems with a taxi driver, contact TransAD.

Walking & Cycling

Cities in the UAE are generally very car-orientated and not designed to encourage walking, especially as daytime temperatures in the summer months reach around 45°C. That said, the relative compactness of Abu Dhabi's main area makes walking and cycling a pleasant way of getting around in the cooler months, and an evening stroll or bike ride along the Corniche is a must. Bear in mind though that many car drivers are not used to pedestrian traffic, so do keep alert when out and about on your own feet or on two wheels. The cycle track at the Corniche is very safe and, for a scenic alternative, Yas Marina Circuit opens to walkers, runners, roller bladers and cyclists on Tuesday nights which is a fun experience. Bikes can be hired at the circuit.

An evening stroll along the Corniche

Places To Stay

If it's opulence you're looking for then you've chosen the right destination. There are few places in the world that offer such jaw-dropping luxury.

The standard of hotels in the emirate is so high that once you've spent a night or two in an Abu Dhabi five-star hotel, you might find five-star hotels in other parts of the world a bit disappointing. Abu Dhabi Tourism & Culture Authority rates hotels from one star to five, but five-star hotels are further classified into silver, gold and platinum. They also plan to take online customer feeback into account to keep standards high.

At present, good quality budget hotels are rare, but the selection of fantastic hotels and resorts might not be as expensive as you think. The initial price quoted, or the 'rack rate', is usually negotiable, and seasonal price fluctuations and special offers may make a stay in one of the palatial properties more affordable. Because restaurants and bars have to be part of a hotel or club to get a licence to serve alcohol, most hotels in the UAE are centres for social activity.

Abu Dhabi City

Most of Abu Dhabi's traditional hotels are on the western end of the island, near the Corniche, but following the opening of several venues in areas such as Al Maqtaa and Yas Island, visitors now have a wide range of choice.

Al Raha Beach Hotel

danathotels.com

02 508 0555 **Map** 1 G4

This comfortable hotel boasts a private beach, several bars and restaurants, as well as easy access to the adjacent mall, airport and Yas Island.

Aloft Abu Dhabi

aloftabudhabi.com

02 654 5000 **Map** 2 A2

Although located at the exhibition centre, Aloft is not a standard business hotel. It has a chic design which spreads to its restaurants, pool, gym and roof bar.

Crowne Plaza Yas Island

ichotelsgroup.com

02 656 3000 **Map** 1 H3

This Yas Island venue sits alongside the Links Championship Golf Course and features 428 rooms and a 25 metre outdoor swimming pool, as well as six bars and restaurants.

Eastern Mangroves Hotel & Spa By Anantara

anantara.com

02 656 1000 **Map** 1 D3

As unique as Anantara's exotic resorts. The city property is aimed at business travellers, but views over the mangroves make it an oasis of calm.

Emirates Palace

kempinski.com

02 690 9000 **Map** 3 A2

This Abu Dhabi landmark boasts 392 opulent rooms and suites. There are 15 outstanding food outlets offering five-star service and guests can enjoy the 1.3km stretch of private beach overlooking an idyllic bay.

Fairmont Bab Al Bahr

fairmont.com

02 654 3333 **Map** 2 D1

The Fairmont Bab Al Bahr relies on minimalism and contemporary design to establish its own form of luxury. A private beach and several top restaurants round out an already impressive package.

Hilton Abu Dhabi

hilton.com

02 681 1900 **Map** 3 A2

Conveniently located near the Corniche and Marina Mall, the Hilton is one of Abu Dhabi's landmark hotels; the hotel's beach club (p.181) is also among the city's best and most popular.

Hyatt Capital Gate Abu Dhabi

hyatt.com

02 596 1234 **Map** 2 A2

Located in the world's 'most leaning' building. The 189 rooms and 22 suites are understated and welcoming, with decor to match those views.

InterContinental Abu Dhabi > *p.iv, 21*

ichotelsgroup.com

02 666 6888 **Map** 3 A3

This hotel offers 390 modern rooms and suites. There is a choice of superb eateries, a gym, outdoor pool, tennis courts and a private beach.

Jumeirah At Etihad Towers

jumeirah.com

02 811 5555 **Map** 3 A2

Towering above Emirates Palace and offering some of the best views in town, Jumeirah's first venture in the capital is on a grand and luxurious scale, from the giant Asian-style lobby to the 382 rooms.

One To One Hotel – The Village

onetoonehotels.com

02 495 2000 **Map** 3 F6

The One To One offers a more personal experience than the big chains. It is close to the airport and it houses a number of very good restaurants.

Park Hyatt Abu Dhabi Hotel & Villas

hyatt.com

02 407 1234 **Map** 1 D1

Laid-back, elegant and luxurious, the Park Hyatt has 306 rooms and four pools sat in landscaped grounds next to a private stretch of wave-swept beach.

The Ritz-Carlton Grand Canal

ritzcarlton.com

02 818 8888 **Map** 2 B7

Located on the waterway that separates Abu Dhabi island from the mainland, this sprawling resort has some of the hottest food and drink tickets in town.

Royal Rose Hotel

royalrosehotel.com

02 762 4000 **Map** 3 F2

A brand new hotel styled with a French 17th century palace in mind. Opulent and grand, the 355 room hotel is high living in the heart of the city.

Shangri-La Hotel, Qaryat Al Beri

shangri-la.com

02 509 8888 **Map** 2 D2

The Shangri-La exudes luxury. The 214 rooms and suites all have private terraces with sea views. It offers a spa, two gyms, private beach and five swimming pools.

The St Regis Saadiyat Island Resort

stregissaadiyatisland.com
02 498 8888 **Map** 1 D1

More California beach retreat than UAE hotel, colonial style rooms offer views over the central pools, restaurant, sandy beach and the Saadiyat Beach golf course.

The Westin Abu Dhabi Golf Resort & Spa

westinabudhabigolfresort.com
02 616 9999 **Map** 1 F4

One of the city's newest hotel offerings, located just off the island, the 172 rooms looking out over the Abu Dhabi Golf Club make it the perfect place for fairway fans.

Yas Viceroy Abu Dhabi

viceroyhotelsandresorts.com
02 656 0000 **Map** 1 H3

This futuristic hotel is now a landmark thanks to its incredible circuit-straddling design. With 499 rooms and suites, views over the Yas Marina Circuit and Yas Marina, it has become a popular choice.

Hotels By Area

Tourist Club Area & Corniche East

The spectacular Abu Dhabi Corniche is the place to be; along with the Tourist Club Area next door, this area forms the main business district but is also a key destination for tourism and leisure. Le Royal Meridien Abu Dhabi is home to 11 different dining options, including Al Fanar: the city's first revolving restaurant (leroyalmeridienabudhabi.com).

The Crowne Plaza is a well-established and well-known property located just a few minutes' walk from the shopping district and beach and offers stunning rooftop views (ichotelsgroup.com).

The Beach Rotana Abu Dhabi boasts some of the city's most popular dining outlets and shoppers will find the direct access to the Abu Dhabi Mall handy (rotana.com). With 12 restaurants, great leisure facilities and a private beach, the Sheraton Abu Dhabi Hotel and Resort is always popular too (sheraton.com).

On the new Maryah Island development across the water, the excellent Rosewood Hotel (rosewoodhotels.com) is a welcome new addition, with a Four Seasons soon to follow.

Even the hotels that cater more specifically to business travellers are good options for tourists, thanks in part to their leisure facilities and restaurants. Good business hotels that double up as leisure destinations include Cristal Hotel (cristalhotelsandresorts.com), Grand Continental Flamingo Hotel (gcfh.ae), and Millennium Hotel Abu Dhabi (millenniumhotels.com).

Corniche West & Al Bateen

This is a neighbourhood of top hotels, attractive parks, a sense of peace and a dash of heritage. It's home to Emirates Palace (kempinski.com), Jumeirah at Etihad Towers (jumeirah.com), the landmark InterContinental (ihg.com) and more affordable offerings such as the Khalidiya Palace Rayhaan (rotana.com).

Between The Bridges & ADNEC

Tucked between Mussafah Bridge and Al Maqtaa Bridge, this area has become one of the capital's most prestigious, thanks to the stylish hotels featuring a host of excellent dining options. The beautiful Shangri-La Qaryat Al Beri Hotel (p.71), with its many acclaimed restaurants and linked Traders Hotel and Souk Qaryat Al Beri, is one of the draws, as is the Fairmont Bab Al Bahr (p.68). Across the water, Ritz-Carlton Grand Canal (p.71) provides ultimate luxury with an expanding choice of restaurants. For ADNEC, the Hyatt Capital Gate (p.69), Aloft (aloftabudhabi.com), Premier Inn Capital Centre (global.premierinn.com) and Cento Capital Centre (rotana.com) provide easy access, as does the Holiday Inn (ihg.com) and new Novotel Al Bustan (novotel.com). The Hilton Capital Grand (hilton.com) adds a more upscale option. Towards the city, the impressive Dusit Thani (dusit.com) is an excellent choice that is central to most places.

Yas Island & Off Abu Dhabi Island

Following the opening of Yas Links Golf Course, Ferrari World Abu Dhabi and Yas Waterworld, Yas Island is now a major leisure destination. Yas Viceroy Abu Dhabi (p.72)), and other accommodation providers followed suit, so there's now a good amount of choice. Centro Yas Island (rotana.com) was the first offering from Rotana's affordable-executive range: large rooms and first-class amenities belie the rates. The Yas Island Rotana features gorgeous decor and superior service, while the Crowne Plaza boasts great views and restaurants. Also on the island are the Park Inn Abu Dhabi – modern, colourful and suitable for those on a smaller budget – and the Radisson Blu Hotel (both radisson.com), which offers fantastic views across the golf course towards the city and a superb, relaxed vibe. Not on the island but in the area are The Westin Abu Dhabi Golf Resort & Spa (p.72) and the Al Raha Beach Hotel (p.67) – also fantastic resort properties.

Saadiyat Island

Saadiyat now has hotels to offer in the form of the sprawling and delightful beach resorts run by St Regis (p.72) and Park Hyatt (p.70). Both offer huge rooms with sweeping beach panoramas and are ideal for ultimate relaxation. More hotels are currently being built on the island, including a Shangri-La.

Hotel Apartments & Hostels

Abu Dhabi is not a budget destination, but a cheaper alternative to staying in a hotel is to rent furnished accommodation on a daily, weekly or monthly basis. Hotel apartments such as the Vision Hotel Apartments (visionhotels.com) are fully furnished and have a maid service, as well as a gym and pool. Alternatively, there are some hostels in Dubai, Sharjah and Fujairah (uaeyha.com).

Further Out

Outside the city, there's plenty to see and luckily the accommodation options have improved greatly over the last few years as new resorts such as Qasr Al Sarab (see p.77) have opened. Al Ain, known as the 'garden city' due to its greenery, is home to several resorts and hotels. Danat Al Ain Resort is a good option for families: set among landscaped gardens, it offers a range of room options, family friendly facilities and several food and beverage outlets (danathotels.com). The Hilton Al Ain is a little closer to the city centre and its restaurants and leisure facilities are popular with local residents too (hilton.com). Al Ain Rotana offers spacious rooms and excellent leisure facilities, as well as a host of popular dining and entertainment options (p.230). The Mercure Grand Jebel Hafeet, meanwhile, enjoys a lofty mountain-top location, lovely views and wonderful leisure facilities, as well as a great pool play area for kids (mercure.com) to while away the hours.

Arabian Nights Village (arabiannightsvillage.com) is a new resort in the middle of the desert, south-west of Abu Dhabi. The Arabic-styled, private detached houses let you enjoy a remote desert stay, with total luxury and no interruptions.

The Danat Resort Jebel Dhanna (danathotels.com) is located 240km west of Abu Dhabi right on the shallow waters of the Gulf. It offers fantastic leisure facilities and a pristine beach, as well as access to the area's biggest attraction, Sir Bani Yas Island (desertislands.com). Also along the coast but a little closer to Abu Dhabi is the Mirfa Hotel (almarfapearlhotels.com).

Desert Escapes

A trip to the desert is a must when in Abu Dhabi. Located a few hours west of the city and further than most visitors usually venture, the region known as Al Gharbia (p.134) boasts stunning scenery. Camping under the stars is one way to experience it all, but if comfort is what you're after, there are a few luxurious alternatives: the following retreats boast breathtaking settings, fine dining and sumptuous spas to make a perfect getaway.

Desert Islands Resort & Spa By Anantara

desertislands.anantara.com
02 801 5400

This resort features 64 rooms, a spa and full access to the Arabian Wildlife Park. The activities include 4WD safaris, hiking, snorkelling and kayaking.

Qasr Al Sarab Desert Resort By Anantara

qasralsarab.anantara.com
02 886 2088

This extraordinary retreat near Liwa features a beautiful pool and an Anantara spa, along with tastefully decorated, Arabian-themed rooms, suites and villas.

Exploring

Explore Abu Dhabi	80
At A Glance	82
Ras Al Akhdar & Breakwater	84
Corniche West	90
Corniche East & Central Abu Dhabi	94
Al Meena & Tourist Club Area	100
Al Safarat, Al Matar & Al Maqtaa	106
Off The Island	112
The Islands	120
Al Ain	126
Al Gharbia	134
Off The Beaten Track	140
Further Out	142
Tours & Sightseeing	150

Explore Abu Dhabi

Abu Dhabi offers activities, sights and excitement without crowds for all visitors. Enjoy the opulent luxury and fascinating heritage of this island city.

Between the calm green gardens, high-rise apartment blocks, elegant fountains, stunning Corniche and luxury villas, is a truly vibrant city. Abu Dhabi is growing rapidly, and its evolution from quiet village to thriving metropolis has been remarkable, a testament to the vision of the late Sheikh Zayed, and the energy and drive of its people.

The high-rise central business district is home to imaginatively designed buildings which provide a dramatic backdrop to the Corniche area. The Corniche itself is designed for play, with beautiful parks, walkways, cycle paths and picnic areas, all bordering the turquoise waters of the Arabian Gulf. Further inland the high-rise buildings make way for beautiful villas, low-rise apartment blocks and quieter, tree-lined streets.

We've listed the must-see sights from museums to heritage sites, parks and beaches on the following pages, and there's also a brief overview of the other emirates (p.142). If you're short of time, or want to explore further afield, an organised tour (p.150) is a great way to make the most of your visit. For more information on exploring the rapidly evolving city, check out the *Abu Dhabi Explorer* or *Abu Dhabi Tourist Map.*

Downtown Abu Dhabi

At A Glance

Heritage Sites

Al Jahili Fort & Park p.130
Al Maqtaa Fort p.108
Heritage Village p.86
Hili Archaeological Gardens p.130
Qasr Al Hosn p.97
Sheikh Zayed Grand Mosque p.108

Museums & Art Galleries

Al Ain National Museum p.129

Parks

Al Khalidiya Public Park p.91
Khalifa Park p.108

Beaches & Beach Parks

Corniche Beach Park p.96

Activities & Leisure

Abu Dhabi Falcon Hospital p.114
Abu Dhabi Golf Club p.114
Abu Dhabi International Marine Sports Club p.86
Abu Dhabi Pottery p.140
Al Forsan International Sports Resort p.115
Freediving UAE p.140

Hili Fun City	p.131
Noukhada Adventure Company	p.141
The Club	p.103
Wadi Adventure	p.131
Women's Handicraft Centre	p.141

Sights & Attractions

Al Ain Camel & Livestock Souk	p.128
Al Ain Oasis	p.129
Al Ain Zoo	p.129
Al Maqam Camel Race Track	p.140
Bahraini Island	p.120
Bateen Dhow Yard	p.91
Desert Islands	p.134
Dhow Harbour	p.103
Emirates Park Zoo	p.116
Futaisi Island	p.120
Green Mubazzarah	p.130
International Fund for Houbara Conservation	p.116
Jebel Dhanna	p.135
Liwa	p.136
Saadiyat Island	p.121
The Souk At Qaryat Al Beri	p.109
Yas Island	p.122
Zayed Sports City	p.109

Ras Al Akhdar & Breakwater

Ras Al Akhdar's pride is the iconic Emirates Palace. Nearby, Breakwater is home to a massive mall, a heritage village and some impressive views.

Ras Al Akhdar is the area at the western tip of Abu Dhabi island. It is dominated by the Emirates Palace hotel (p.68), reputedly the most expensive hotel ever built. Bakarat Gallery (02 690 8950) is located here and includes interesting exhibits of Islamic and international art. Emirates Palace should be on every tourist's must-see list; the impressive hotel houses a number of restaurants and cafes and you don't have to be a guest to enjoy a lovely meal here.

Adding to the high-end hotel offering in this area is the Jumeirah at Etihad Towers, which is also well worth a visit for its excellent outlets or the stunning views from the higher floors.

Ras Al Akhdar's other main attractions are

Record Breakwater

One of the most famous landmarks on the Breakwater is the enormous flagpole next to the Heritage Village. For some time this was the tallest unsupported flagpole in the world (123m), until Jordan erected an even taller one (126m) in 2003. It's now the fifth tallest, since Tajikistan flew their flag from a 163m high unsupported pole in 2011.

the Corniche and the Breakwater. You could rent a bicycle and pedal your way up and down the Corniche to soak up the atmosphere while enjoying the gorgeous scenery and stopping for a bite or a drink at one of the outlets. Contact Byky (q8byky.com) for details on the rental locations and prices. Breakwater is an area of reclaimed land connected by a causeway to the Corniche. The beachfront walkways are an extension of the Corniche development and offer some spectacular views of the city. Marina Mall (p.208), one of the capital's largest, is also located here, so you can indulge in some retail therapy if the summer weather gets too hot to stay outside.

The fascinating Heritage Village (p.86) overlooks the Corniche. It is run by the Emirates Heritage Club and gives an interesting insight into the way life used to be in this part of the world. For example, you can test the effectiveness of the earliest form of air conditioning by standing under the wind tower in the traditional houses made of barasti (dried palm leaves). There are also loads of great photo opportunities here, such as the chance to get up close and personal with an Arabian horse or a camel.

Once you've wandered around outside, head into the air-conditioned museum which houses a collection of local artefacts from days gone by. The collection includes coffee pots, diving tools, Holy Qurans, jewellery, weapons and garments.

After visiting the village, sample some typical Arabic cuisine at the beachside restaurant (p.241). It has a great view of the Corniche, and it's close to a pleasant kids' play area.

Abu Dhabi International Marine Sports Club

02 681 5566

Nr Marina Mall, Breakwater

adimsc.ae

The Abu Dhabi International Marine Sports Club is the organising body for local and international powerboat events, traditional watersports and jetski races. In addition, the club has a marina with serviced berths, workshops and a showroom which stocks marine sports and fishing accessories. Watersports from kayaking to powerboating are supported here. **Map** 3 B1

Heritage Village

02 681 4455

Nr Marina Mall, Breakwater

For an interesting glimpse into the country's past, a trip to the Heritage Village offers a chance to see what life was

People's Palace

Despite being one of Abu Dhabi's more exclusive venues, Emirates Palace hosts a number of events each year which are open to the public, including large-scale concerts in the garden that have featured international stars from Andrea Bocelli to The Killers. It is also the venue for some of the Abu Dhabi Film Festival screenings and events, and hosts performances from the Abu Dhabi Classics programme in its auditorium. Check askexplorer.com to find out about upcoming events.

like in Abu Dhabi long before the discovery of oil and the subsequent development. Learn more about traditional crafts directly from local craftsmen who are happy to show you how it's done. It is a fantastic place to shop for souvenirs, like authentic pottery or exotic spices. Falconry displays are held on Thursday evenings during the summer months. It is open daily from 09:00 until 17:00, except Fridays when the hours are 15:30 to 21:00. **Map** 3 C1

If you only do one thing in...

Ras Al Akhdar & Breakwater

Take in the views of the city skyline from Breakwater.

Best for...

Sightseeing: Wander around the Heritage Village (p.86) at leisure and observe local men and women sharing their skills in traditional crafts.

Eating: Enjoy authentic Arabic cuisine at a Breakwater restaurant, sample sumptuous sushi at Il Porto (p.255), or treat yourself to an afternoon tea in Emirates Palace (p.68).

Families: The Heritage Village (p.86) is the closest you'll get to travelling back in time with its displays of Bedouin life.

Relaxation: Pick up picnic supplies at Marina Mall (p.208), then grab a spot along the beach before it gets too busy.

Shopping: Pay a whirlwind visit to Marina Mall's 250 shops and revolving restaurant.

Clockwise from top left: Marina Mall, exhibits in the Heritage Village, Emirates Palace

Corniche West

With two of the city's top hotels, a number of beautiful parks and an air of tranquillity, this is one of the capital's most affluent areas.

In the west of the city, the Corniche begins at the end of the causeway to the Breakwater. Recently redeveloped, the Corniche is an attractive esplanade with pleasant parks and green areas dotted along it. The Hilton Abu Dhabi (hilton.com) stands on the land side while the Hiltonia Beach Club has pride of place on the sea side. The Hilton is one of the city's older hotels but is still one of its most luxurious and popular. Its bars and restaurants are always busy, so if you're planning an evening out it's best to book ahead.

Al Bateen is a sought-after residential area and you'll find great parks and a number of coffee shops here. The Khalidiyah Public Park and the Khalidiya Children's Garden (ladies and children only) are well frequented by picnickers in the evenings and at weekends and well worth the visit. Al Bateen is also home to the InterContinental Abu Dhabi (p.69), another of the city's well-established luxury hotels, which houses the highly-rated Fish Market and Chamas Brazilian Churrascaria (p.249) restaurants.

Further along the coast are the Bateen Wharf, Bateen jetty (with a number of marine supply stores around it) and the Bateen dhow yard. A visit to the dhow yard is essential, not just to absorb the evocative smells of freshly cut African and Indian teak, but also to watch craftsmen build magnificent dhows and racing vessels using age-old techniques. These wooden vessels can still be seen during dhow races off the Corniche or plying the trade routes around the Gulf and across the Indian Ocean. Al Bateen Wharf, the capital's oldest residential area, is being redeveloped and some new residences are now open. Other parts of the area can, however, be explored, offering the chance to see some beautiful traditional architecture – most notably the heritage centre built by Abu Dhabi Heritage Club.

Al Khalidiya Public Park

Al Khaleej Al Arabi St, Al Khalidiyah

Taking up a whole block, this large park is popular with families. It has a variety of play areas, with equipment suitable for toddlers and older children. Its lovely grassy areas are great for lounging, with a number of large trees providing excellent shade. You can pick up picnic supplies at Abu Dhabi Cooperative Society on the south side of the park. **Map** 3 C3

Bateen Dhow Yard

Al Bateen

The skilled craftsmen in this fascinating boat yard use traditional techniques to construct the dhows, which are still used for racing and for trade throughout the Gulf region and the Indian Ocean. Visit in the early evening and not only will you be able to get some wonderful photos of the sun setting behind the hulls, you may also be able to talk to the craftsmen – if they are not too busy they are usually happy to share an insight into their traditional craft. **Map** 3 A4

54

If you only do one thing in... Corniche West

Enjoy the seaside – relax on the beach, stroll the Corniche or chat to boat builders at the dhow yard.

Best for...

Eating & Drinking: Head to Al Mawal (p.261) at the Hilton for a lively Lebanese meal with entertainment.

Families: Khalidiya Children's Garden is a ladies and children only park with rides and play equipment.

Relaxation: Meander along the Corniche or check yourself in for a leisurely day at Hiltonia Beach Club where you can enjoy swimming pools, a private beach and alfresco dining.

Shopping: Khalidiyah Mall (p.206) and Al Bateen Mall (02 666 1222) house a good variety of stores and entertainment for kids.

Sightseeing: Arrive at Bateen Dhow Yard before sunset and wander round chatting to the craftsmen. Get your camera out as the sun goes down for some great shots of the imposing hulls of the dhows.

Clockwise from top left: Al Bateen Marina, racing dhow, traditional architecture

Corniche East & Central Abu Dhabi

With the well-kept parks of the Corniche sandwiched between the clear blue waters of the gulf and the city's high-rises, this is an area of contrasts.

The redevelopment of Abu Dhabi's iconic Corniche involved the reclaiming of a large strip of land and the creation of a number of new parks and attractions. The high-rise buildings which overlook it were once only separated from the sea by a six-lane road, but now a lush strip of greenery sits on the other side. An evening stroll along the Corniche should be part of every visit to the capital – this is where many of the city's residents come to meet, have picnics and relax, especially in the evenings and at weekends.

This area is generally seen as the city centre or main business district. Among the high-rises is the oldest building in the capital, the Qasr Al Hosn (the Old Fort, also known as the White Fort or Fort Palace), which dates back to 1793. It was the official residence of the rulers of Abu Dhabi for many years. The fort itself is not currently open to the public.

Sheikh Hamdan bin Mohammed Street (known as Hamdan Street) is a haven for avid shoppers, with local and international stores sharing the limelight with a number of independent stores, restaurants and entertainment venues. At the end of Hamdan Street is the Marks & Spencer mall (Fotouh Al Khair Centre, p.204), which houses several international stores and a great cafe. Further up Hamdan

Street is the World Trade Center. The Central Market souk was the first part to open, but in 2013 the World Trade Center Mall opened its doors to the delight of shoppers. The high rise buildings add some real glamour to the area.

Gold is an excellent purchase while you are in the UAE, and you'll find plenty of it in the many jewellery shops lining the street before the Liwa Centre (p.207). So much gold is packed into the windows of these shops that at night the dazzling yellow glow from the displays spills out onto the pavements. The Hamdan Centre (p.206) is something of an institution and should be a stop on every visitor's tour. It is packed with small shops selling everything from souvenirs to (not entirely authentic) designer label clothes. It's also a great place to test your bargaining skills.

The Madinat Zayed Shopping Centre & Gold Centre (p.207) is quieter than the other big malls, but it does come to life a little in the evenings. There are some bigger shops here, but it is especially worth a visit for the smaller shops selling perfumes, clothes, fabric

Intrepid Explorers

While we like to think that we have covered every inch of Abu Dhabi, filtered out the missable and highlighted the unmissable, you may feel differently. So if you think we've left something out then we would love to hear your suggestions. Maybe it's an undiscovered heritage site or a fabulous neighbourhood restaurant that you want to shout about. Whatever it may be, log on to askexplorer.com to fill in our reader response form.

and haberdashery. The Gold Centre has some of the region's largest jewellery stores and is a great place to buy gold. If you want the classic souvenir of your name written in Arabic on a gold necklace, this is where to get it.

Some of the capital's top hotels are in this area, including Le Royal Meridien (05 674 2020), Sofitel (02 813 777) and the Sheraton Abu Dhabi Hotel & Resort (02 677 3333) all of which have popular bars and restaurants. While there are plenty of fine-dining options within easy reach, don't miss out on delicious and authentic cuisine served at the many independent restaurants that line these streets – good food at really great prices, with a side order of atmosphere.

New Corniche

The Corniche should not be confused with the New Corniche (aka the Eastern Corniche), which runs along the north eastern side of the island and is also known as the Eastern Ring Road. It too has had a face lift, and is a popular place for barbecues, picnics and a spot of fishing. The area near the Dolphin Fountains is the perfect spot for a family game of football or cricket.

Corniche Beach Park

Corniche Road West,
Al Khubeirah

This two-kilometre stretch of pristine, white-sand beach has excellent leisure facilities and there is also a selection of coffee and fast food outlets to choose from near the main entrance. The park is split with separate family and men's entrances, and there is space for everyone. Admission is Dhs.10.
Map 3 B2

Qasr Al Hosn

Shk Zayed First St, Markaziya West abudhabi.ae

The Old Fort is the oldest building in Abu Dhabi, dating back to 1793. It was the official residence of the rulers of Abu Dhabi. The area is currently being redeveloped by Abu Dhabi Tourism & Culture Authority (adach.ae) and there are plans to reopen the fort as a museum and public monument.

Map 3 E3

Clockwise from top left: Qasr Al Hosn, white sands along the Corniche, Abu Dhabi Corniche

If you only do one thing in...
Corniche East & Central Abu Dhabi

Tap into the heart of the city with an evening stroll along the Corniche.

Best for...

Eating & Drinking: Enjoy cheap chow at a pavement cafe, soaking up the atmosphere as the city starts winding down.

Families: Spend a day beside the seaside with sandcastles and ice creams at Corniche Beach Park.

Relaxation: Take time out along the Corniche. In the evenings, it's a great place to mingle with residents enjoying a bit of leisure time.

Shopping: Haggle away at the Hamdan Centre (p.206) where you can engage in the traditional art of bargaining or check out the architectural wonders of Central Market.

Sightseeing: Head for the Gold Souk (p.207) – the sheer quantity of gold on offer is amazing.

Al Meena & Tourist Club Area

Amid bustling high-rises, you'll find some of the city's best hotels and recreational facilities; it's no wonder that this is where fun-seekers gather.

Al Meena is the name given to the whole of the north-western tip of Abu Dhabi island, while the Tourist Club Area (named after a now demolished recreational club) is the area from around the Beach Rotana hotel down to Al Salam Street. The site of the old Tourist Club is currently being redeveloped, but otherwise this bustling area is packed with high-rise apartment blocks, luxury hotels and top shopping spots.

The Tourist Club Area's main draws are Abu Dhabi Mall (p.200), which was Abu Dhabi's second mega mall complete with multi-screen cinema and cafes; the Abu Dhabi Co-operative Society (p.200), for more chances to shop; and the Khalifa Centre (p.206), just behind the old Co-op, which is packed with souvenir shops. Some of Abu Dhabi's top hotels are in this area. They are known for their great restaurants and lounges, making the streets around them very popular in the evenings. The Beach Rotana Abu Dhabi is linked to Abu Dhabi Mall – very handy if you're weighed down with shopping bags – and is home to the ever popular Trader Vic's (p.274) as well as many other great restaurants. The Culinary Village at Le Meridien, just down the road, also has a number of good restaurants. You can choose between French, Indian or excellent Italian at Pappagallo (02 644 6666), which has a

Abu Dhabi Mall

Beach Rotana Hotel & Towers
Abu Dhabi Mall

picturesque terrace. For something a little lower key head to the restaurants in and around Abu Dhabi Marina & Yacht Club (02 644 0300). This aging establishment is a little spit and sawdust but you're guaranteed a fun night out.

Abu Dhabi Airport City Terminal is across the road from the Beach Rotana hotel (rotana.com). Buses leave on a regular basis to Abu Dhabi International Airport, and most airlines have check-in facilities here too.

Al Meena begins as an area of high-rises and ends at Port Zayed (a working port). Once you leave the high-rises behind, the area on the right is best known for the Carpet Souk (p.197). Most of what is sold is mass-produced but there are gems to be found if you know what you're looking for.

The Club, one of the capital's most popular health and beach clubs, is also here but unfortunately is for members only. To the left, past the Customs building, is Port Zayed. This working port is home to the Fish Souk (p.198) – the odours emanating from here can politely be described as 'colourful'. The adjacent Vegetable Souk is probably a more pleasantly fragrant way to experience the hustle and bustle of a traditional market (p.196). Further on, you can browse through an impressive range of plants and household

Picture Perfect

***Images of Abu Dhabi and the UAE*, available in leading bookshops, supermarkets and at askexplorer.com/shop, captures the inspiring wonders of the city, from architectural marvels to the breathtaking landscapes. It's a perfect memento of your holiday.**

goods imported directly from Iran at the aptly named Iranian Souk. The Mina Centre, in the heart of the port, is a huge mall with a great bookshop (Jarir Bookstore), a supermarket and a children's amusement centre. From Al Meena you can access the islands via the Sheikh Khalifa highway, an impressive stretch of tarmac that crosses picturesque mangroves before linking with the mainland beyond Yas Island. The highway is also the quickest route into downtown Abu Dhabi if you're visiting from north of the city.

The Club

Mina Zayed Free Port
02 673 1111
the-club.com

An Abu Dhabi institution, The Club has been going for nearly 50 years. This leisure facility is one of the most successful expat clubs in the capital, and guests must be signed in by a member. It has excellent facilities and it often puts on plays and concerts not found anywhere else in the city. **Map** 1 C2

Dhow Harbour

Nr Al Dhafra Restaurant, Al Meena

The Dhow Harbour is particularly atmospheric at sunset when the fleet returns. The harbour is also the starting point for a number of dinner cruises, with the one run by the Al Dhafra seafood restaurant (p.241) being very popular – it sails along the Corniche every evening. Even though there are some beautiful sights in the port, no photography is allowed in the area as Port Zayed is a working port with security restrictions in place. **Map** 3 G1

If you only do one thing in...

Al Meena & Tourist Club Area

Put your best bartering skills into practice at the souks.

Best for...

Eating & Drinking: Head to the Beach Rotana Abu Dhabi (rotana.com) and enjoy a delicious buffet lunch at Rosebuds Restaurant & Terrace.

Families: Set sail from the Dhow Harbour for a tranquil dinner cruise organised by Al Dhafra seafood restaurant (p.241).

Shopping: Hit the retail jackpot with a trip around the 200 shops inside the Abu Dhabi Mall. With four storeys and around 26,000 visitors daily, this is an essential destination if you like shopping.

Sightseeing: Peruse the catch of the day at the Fish Market before browsing through the myriad of colours and shapes at the Vegetable Market. Select a rug at the nearby Carpet Souk and then head to the Dhow Harbour to soak up the atmosphere created by traditional wooden dhows and their exotic cargo.

Top: Beach Rotana Abu Dhabi; Bottom: Carpet Souk

Al Safarat, Al Matar & Al Maqtaa

The southern end of the island boasts some of Abu Dhabi's most iconic landmarks. Here you can explore the emirate's heritage and look to its future.

This end of the island is currently undergoing major development, with several tourist, residential and commercial projects underway. Al Safarat is dominated by the Abu Dhabi National Exhibition Centre (ADNEC), a newly redeveloped facility used for major international business events and public festivals such as Summer In Abu Dhabi, a family bonanza that runs in July and August. Located adjacent to ADNEC, the Aloft hotel offers a number of restaurants and bars (p.67); the world's 'most leaning tower', Capital Gate, houses a Hyatt hotel (p.69).

Al Safarat is also home to Zayed Sports City, which has a football stadium, ice rink and bowling alley, not to mention a tennis stadium that hosts the Mubadala World Tennis Championship (p.175) every winter. Access to the ice rink costs Dhs.15 (Dhs.40 for skate hire); call 02 403 4333 for more info. Old Airport Garden, near Zayed Sports City, is a lovely park with lots of shade and loads for kids to do.

Al Matar, on the other side of Airport Road, is dominated by the Khalifa Park. One of the city's newest parks, its gardens have an international flavour and are set amid canals, lakes, fountains and waterfalls. There are play areas for children, picnic spots, and the indoor Murjan Splash Park – fun for younger children, especially during the hot summer months.

Al Maqtaa is named after the heavily renovated Al Maqtaa Fort, which stands guard over the island. This area is dominated by the Sheikh Zayed bin Sultan Al Nahyan Mosque, known locally as the Grand Mosque, and the Armed Forces Officers Club & Hotel. The massive mosque, which holds up to 30,000 worshippers, is a major landmark and non-Muslims can visit it during set hours. The Armed Forces Officers Club & Hotel has some excellent recreational facilities, including two indoor shooting galleries and a good selection of restaurants. New to this area is the sprawling Ritz-Carlton Grand Canal (p.71) resort, which has more than 500 rooms, suites and villas, as well as a handful of excellent restaurants and bars.

The area on the mainland side of the creek is known as Between The Bridges (it sits between Mussafah Bridge and Al Maqtaa Bridge). It is noted for large villas and compounds, but its focal point is the Qaryat Al Beri development (see map 2 D2). This complex is styled on traditional Arabic architecture and is home to a souk, the deluxe Shangri-La hotel (p.71) and Traders Hotel. Excellent leisure facilities lie within the Shangri-La including Bord Eau French restaurant (p.249), exclusive Pearls & Caviar (p.267), and CHI spa. Across the creek from the Qaryat Al Beri is an ornate Persian-influenced mosque. This small turquoise-blue structure is not open to the public for tours, but you can admire the craftsmanship from outside.

Next to the Traders Hotel is the Fairmont Bab Al Bahr (p.68). Among its attractions are Marco Pierre White Steakhouse & Grill (p.261) and Frankie's (p.252).

Al Maqtaa Fort

Nr Maqtaa Bridge, Al Maqtaa visitabudhabi.ae

Your first glimpse of the monument will likely be as you approach the Al Maqtaa Bridge towards Abu Dhabi island. The 200 year-old, heavily renovated fort stands at the edge of the island and was built to fend off bandits. It is one of the few remaining of its kind in Abu Dhabi and, while you can't access the island on which it stands, it's a great photo opportunity and provides a wonderful contrast to the modern bridge. **Map** 2 D1

Khalifa Park

02 449 0346

Nr Al Bateen Airport, Al Matar adm.gov.ae

This landmark park has gardens set in a landscape of canals and fountains. Train tours of the park are available if you don't want to cover it on foot. It is home to kids' playgrounds, picnic facilities, an outdoor auditorium, and even has a free time travel ride that explores the UAE's history. During cooler months, a community market sees stalls set up in the park every evening. A host of activity programmes for kids are regularly run at the park as well. **Map** 2 C1

Sheikh Zayed Grand Mosque

02 441 6444

Shk Rashid Bin Saeed Al Maktoum St, Al Maqtaa szgmc.ae

A visit to this beautiful place of worship is a must – not only is it one of Abu Dhabi's most iconic buildings but it is also one of the few mosques open to non-Muslims. Public access is from Saturday to Thursday, between 09:00 and 22:00 (except during the call to prayer and prayer times). Strict dress codes are in place so make sure you wear long, loose-fitting garments covering your wrists and ankles. Women must wear an abaya; these are provided free of charge at the mosque. Guided tours are available for groups of 30 or more and must be booked a week in advance. For group bookings and more information visit the website. **Map** 2 C2

The Souk At Qaryat Al Beri

02 558 1670

Qaryat Al Beri Complex, Al Maqtaa soukqaryatalberi.com

The centrepiece of the Qaryat Al Beri complex, the atmospheric souk is a modern take on a traditional Arabian market. With regional and international brands, it's a good destination for shopping, and the canal-side alfresco dining options make it a popular hangout. Arabic gondolas slowly meander along a series of waterways and canals through the unique architecture and lush gardens. Left Bank (02 558 1680) is a great destination for sundowners with a backdrop of impressive Grand Mosque views. **Map** 2 D1

Zayed Sports City

02 403 4200

Al Khaleej Al Arabi St, Al Madina Al Riyadiya zsc.ae

Zayed Sports City is a huge complex including a football/multi-purpose stadium with seating for up to 43,000 people, an ice rink, a 40-lane bowling centre, and new padel tennis courts. The ice rink is one of the best places to go to beat the summer heat, but there are also a variety of other facilities including tennis, video games, gyms and a choice of restaurants. **Map** 2 B2

If you only do one thing in...

Al Safarat, Al Matar & Al Maqtaa

Learn about Islamic prayer rituals on the Sheikh Zayed Grand Mosque tour.

Best for...

Eating & Drinking: Enjoy a delicious lunch at the Ritz-Carlton Grand Canal or at one of the area's independent street restaurants.

Families: Escape from the heat at Zayed Sports City, where you and the kids can enjoy ice skating, bumper cars, video games and fast food.

Relaxation: Take a leisurely stroll or ride the park train and tour Khalifa Park. Head to Maqtaa Bridge for sunset photos of the 200-year-old Maqtaa Fort.

Shopping: Shop till you drop at the Souk at Qaryat Al Beri. Reward yourself with a pit stop at a waterside cafe in evocative surroundings.

Sightseeing: The vast but elegant Sheikh Zayed Grand Mosque makes a great photo opportunity.

Clockwise from top: Sheikh Zayed Grand Mosque, Zayed Stadium, Al Maqtaa Fort

Off The Island

Away from the city centre, mainland Abu Dhabi is home to newly-developed areas and leisure facilities which are worth travelling further afield to explore.

Al Raha Beach lines the Dubai-Abu Dhabi highway on the approach to Abu Dhabi. The unmissable Aldar headquarters, shaped like a contact lens, towers over the area; on a clear day the reflections of the coastline in the building's mirrored face are quite impressive. The area is still partially under development but a shopping mall and Al Raha Beach Hotel (p.67) are open. The hotel's eateries include Azur and Sevilla restaurants, and day passes can be purchased for beach access. Al Raha Mall has two cinemas and numerous shops, restaurants and cafes.

Nearby, Abu Dhabi Golf Club has some of the city's best golf facilities and a challenging championship course. It's also where you'll find the new Westin Abu Dhabi Golf resort, with its numerous leisure facilities and dining outlets. More activities are on

Green Shoots

Near Al Raha Beach and the airport, Abu Dhabi's flagship green project, Masdar City, is taking shape. Eventually it will be one of the world's most sustainable cities, powered by renewable energy. The Masdar Institute of Science & Technology is already up and running. Find out more about the project at masdar.ae.

hand at Al Forsan International Sports Resort (p.115), where everything from archery to off-road racing is on offer.

Just beyond Al Raha and towards the airport is Al Ghazal Golf Club (p.160), a testing sand golf course which is home to the World Sand Golf Championship. Also near the airport is Abu Dhabi Falcon Hospital, where you can attend a fascinating falconry tour (see below) or take a guided tour of the animal hospital. Staying on the wildlife theme, a little further along the Dubai-Abu Dhabi Highway is the popular Emirates Park Zoo (p.116).

Abu Dhabi Falcon Hospital

02 575 5155

Nr Abu Dhabi International Airport, Off Sweihan Rd, Al Shamkha

falconhospital.com

Falconry is a national sport in the UAE and the two-hour guided tour available at the hospital provides a unique opportunity to learn about the impressive creatures. The guided tour, which needs to be booked online ahead of time, is conducted twice daily from Sunday to Thursday (falconhospital.com). Also on this site is the Animal Shelter (abudhabianimalshelter.com). **Map** 1 K5

Abu Dhabi Golf Club

02 558 8990

Khalifa City

adgolfclub.com

This club has excellent facilities including a par 72 championship course, a practice bunker, a driving range, a short game area and a golf academy. The club hosts the

Wakeboarding at Al Forsan International Sports Resort

annual Abu Dhabi Golf Championship, a stop on the PGA European Tour. Facilities are open to non-members on a 'pay and play' basis. Golf carts are mandatory but come with cooler box and impressive GPS navigation. **Map** 1 F4

Al Forsan International Sports Resort 02 556 8555

Nr Abu Dhabi Golf Club & Resort,
Khalifa City alforsan.com

Opened in 2011, Al Forsan is now becoming something of a Disneyland for extreme sports fans living in the UAE. The site offers some great paintballing fields, clay pigeon shooting

and archery, go-karting and off-roading circuits and horse riding, but its pieces-de-resistance are without doubt the world-class cable boarding facilities. Both pro and beginner equipment, including lifejackets and helmets, are provided at the entrance and the staff are more than willing to give helpful tips to get you up and riding. **Map** 1 G5

Emirates Park Zoo

02 501 0000
35km from Abu Dhabi, Al Bahya
emiratesparkzoo.com

Offers children the chance to get up close to their favourite animals, combining learning with touch. There are a number of interactive attractions, while the five-acre zoo houses peacocks, ostriches, ibex, camels, horses, raccoons, ferrets, and exotic fish and birds, with anacondas and hippos soon to be added to the 2,000 species already on display. An equestrian school is also set to open on site in the near future. The park is open every day. **Map** 1 K1

International Fund For Houbara Conservation > *p.v, 117*

02 693 4455
National Avian Research Centre, Al Dhafra
houbarafund.org

A global organisation dedicated to the restoration and preservation of the Houbara bustard, an endangered bird which has migrated past the Arabian Peninsula for centuries. The centre in Abu Dhabi, located in Sweihan, some 60km from the city, focuses on the breed and release programmes, and the organisation runs tours of its facilities to explain all about the Houbara bustard, its importance and the role the IFHC plays. **Map** 1 C3

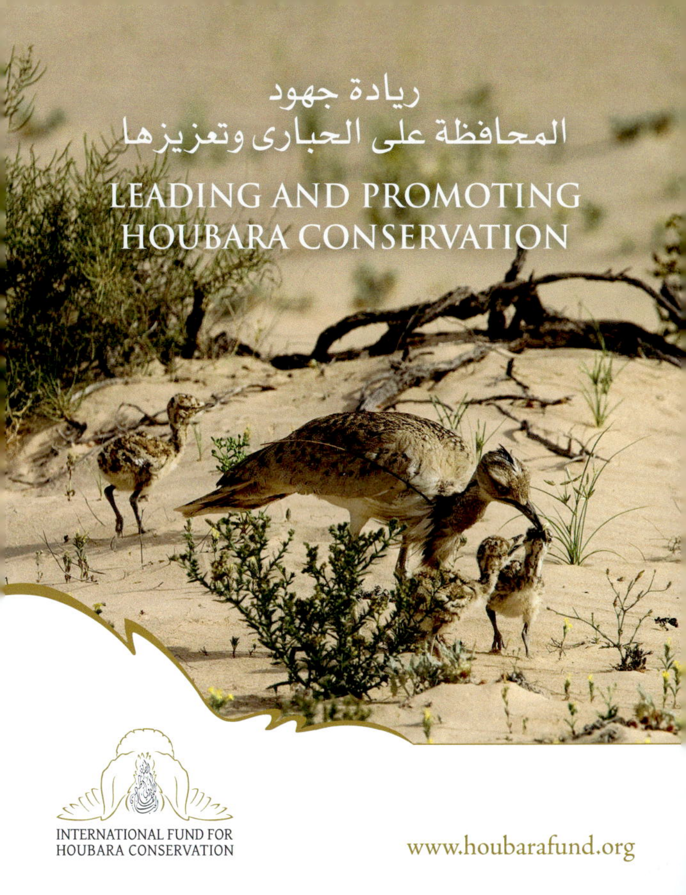
ريادة جهود
المحافظة على الحبارى وتعزيزها
LEADING AND PROMOTING
HOUBARA CONSERVATION
INTERNATIONAL FUND FOR
HOUBARA CONSERVATION
www.houbarafund.org

If you only do one thing in...
Off The Island

Enjoy a poolside lunch under shady palm trees at La Piscine, Al Raha Beach Hotel.

Best for...

Eating & Drinking: Sip a cocktail in the Lemon & Lime Lounge with breathtaking views of the golf course, at Westin Abu Dhabi Golf Resort; or enjoy an Arabian night at its Moroccan restaurant, Agadir.

Families: Spend a leisurely morning on Al Raha Beach Hotel's private stretch of sand, then take a short drive to admire the white tigers and black tip sharks at Emirates Park Zoo.

Relaxation: Opt for a round of golf at Abu Dhabi Golf Club's championship course.

Sightseeing: Have your photo taken with a falcon at the Abu Dhabi Falcon Hospital (p.114).

Abu Dhabi Golf Club

The Islands

Many of Abu Dhabi's hidden treasures are just a short boat ride away, so take to the seas and explore the islands scattered along the coastline.

More than 200 islands pepper the coastal waters of Abu Dhabi and many can be easily accessed either by road or boat. The islands vary in size, and the majority are flat, sandy and uninhabited. The waters around the islands are rich in marine life, and you may be lucky enough to encounter humpbacked dolphins or endangered dugongs on your trip.

Bahraini Island

40 minutes off the Abu Dhabi coast

You'll need to charter a private boat for the 40 minute journey to Bahraini Island but the journey is worth it to spend the day on its unspoiled beaches or at the wildlife sanctuary, and you may be able to spot dolphins en route. Tour companies such as Belevari Marine (02 643 1494, belevari.com) can tailor a day of island hopping for you.

Futaisi Island

5km south of Abu Dhabi Island

Futaisi Island is famed for its wildlife, including turtles and some rare species, an authentic Arabian fort, traditional mosque and mangrove lagoon. A morning boat service (02 666 6601) departs from Al Bateen Marina, returning late afternoon. Overnight chalet accommodation is available.

The Yas Viceroy

Saadiyat Island

500m north of Abu Dhabi

02 406 1400

saadiyat.ae

Abu Dhabi's principal development, Saadiyat Island (saadiyat.ae), translates as 'island of happiness'. The project will feature seven different districts with 29 hotels, three marinas, two golf courses (one of which is already open) and 19 kilometres of beach front. The Cultural District will be the hub of the project with several museums and arts centres, including the Sheikh Zayed National Museum and Abu Dhabi branches

of the Guggenheim and Louvre. All three museums are scheduled to open in the next couple of years, but the Manarat Al Saadiyat (saadiyat.ae) is already open and houses temporary art exhibitions. Also open are the Saadiyat Beach Golf Club (sbgolfclub.ae) and the Monte-Carlo Beach Club (montecarlobeachclub.ae), while the first hotels, The St Regis and Park Hyatt, have also opened their rather splendid doors. **Map** 1 D1

Yas Island > *p.ii-iii, IFC*

North-east of Abu Dhabi yasisland.ae

An island east of Abu Dhabi city centre, Yas has been built up with hotels, infrastructure and Yas Marina Circuit, which opened just in time to host Abu Dhabi's first Formula 1 grand prix in 2009. The 5.6 kilometre track stands out for its unique design which actually runs right through the island's flagship, Yas Viceroy, giving about 250 very lucky VIPs envious views of the proceedings from the bridge on race weekend. What's more, the marina is incorporated into the circuit, so that the yachting crowd can not only make grand entrances but can view the race from their boats. The other 50,000 F1 fans with more modest means can still enjoy thrilling racing moments – the grandstand was designed to offer the best views of any F1 venue.

Racing is only part of the draw of Abu Dhabi's F1 weekend: the end of each racing day brings big pop performances, with Jamiroquai, Prince, Beyoncé, Kanye West, Aerosmith, Kings of Leon and Paul McCartney all having performed in the outdoor du Arena. There are other concerts throughout the year too; Shakira, Madonna, Jay Z, Rolling Stones and Snoop Dogg have all come to town. See thinkflash.ae for more information and to buy tickets. The circuit itself is also open year-round, with attractions such as karting and drag racing available to book (p.170).

The refurbished Yas Marina is now full of excellent restaurants too, and coupled to the bars and eateries at Yas Plaza's hotels, the island is an evening destination in itself.

The world's biggest indoor theme park, Ferrari World Abu Dhabi(p.170), is located right next to the circuit. It features the fastest rollercoaster on the planet amongst its 20 rides and attractions. If that's not enough, then nearby you'll also find the new Yas Waterworld (p.168). The latest water park in a country that has some of the best in the world has managed to raise the bar even higher. Based on an Arabian tale involving a lost pearl, it combines touches of the traditional with the very latest in water entertainment and technology. As well as kids' pools, a lazy river and an interactive pearl diving attraction, the park has some white-knuckle fun in the form of a suspended rollercoaster with integrated water guns, a six-person hydromagnetic tornado ride, a mammoth 'watercoaster', the region's first aqualoop and many more.

The Yas Links golf course opened in March 2010, and the spectacular seaside setting has attracted plenty of attention, not to mention top-golfers, to the island since then. Finally, the Yas Mall is set to open to the public in 2014, adding some top-notch retail therapy to the list of the island's offerings. **Map** 1 H2

If you only do one thing in...
The Islands

Get up close with nature – there is fascinating flora and fauna to be discovered in the water and on dry land – or explore man-made wonders on Yas Island and Saadiyat Island.

Best for...

Families: Head out to Ferrari World (p.170) and Yas Waterworld (p.168) for a day of family fun and thrilling rides.

Relaxation: Catch the morning boat to Futaisi Island, where you can hire bikes or take a horseback or a minibus tour to explore the island's heritage sites including a renovated fort and a mosque. Explore untouched natural habitats and keep a look out for sea eagles, turtles and gazelles. Spend the afternoon relaxing on the beach.

Sightseeing: Drive the Sheikh Khalifa Highway and survey the changing Abu Dhabi landscape. Check up on the progress of Abu Dhabi's island mega projects, admire the futuristic architecture of Yas Viceroy Abu Dhabi, and cross mangroves and coastal lagoons, taking in stunning views of unspoilt natural habitats.

Clockwise from top: Yas Marina, Ferrari World, The Yas Viceroy

Al Ain

The lush 'garden city' of the UAE lies in the shadow of the craggy Jebel Hafeet mountain and is surrounded by imposing red sand dunes.

Al Ain is the capital of the eastern region and Abu Dhabi emirate's second city. Its greenery and status as the birthplace and childhood home of Sheikh Zayed bin Sultan Al Nahyan, the former (and much-loved) ruler of the UAE, gives it a special place in the hearts and minds of the people.

It takes 90 minutes to drive from Abu Dhabi to Al Ain, but, in the pre-oil days, the journey took five days by camel. Most tour companies offer excursions to this fascinating city that straddles the border with the Sultanate of Oman; the UAE side is known as Al Ain and the Oman side as Buraimi. Fortresses around the city, 18 in all, illustrate Al Ain's importance on the ancient trade route from Oman to the Arabian Gulf, and there is evidence of the area having been inhabited for at least the past 7,000 years. The city's archaeological legacy is of such significance that Al Ain is on the tentative list of UNESCO World Heritage Sites.

Throughout his life, Sheikh Zayed pursued his vision of creating a desert oasis by initiating a series of 'greening' projects. As a result, Al Ain's seven natural oases are now surrounded by tree-lined streets and beautiful urban parks. The main Al Ain Oasis is home to palm plantations, many of which are working farms. The palms provide welcome shade and a haven from the bustle of the city but, if you go exploring in the plantations, it is best to stick to the paved areas that weave between the walled-in farms. The Old Prison is also worth a visit for the stunning view of the surrounding town and oasis. The structure is a lone square turret in the centre of a gravel courtyard, surrounded by high walls. Admittance is a bit hit and miss but if you visit with a tour you should be fine.

Al Ain's unique archaeological heritage and history is displayed at Al Ain Museum, on the edge of the main oasis. It has an interesting collection of photographs along with Bedouin jewellery, instruments, and a reconstruction of a traditional majlis. The archaeological section houses finds from nearby Hili Gardens, and it's helpful to visit the museum before heading out to the gardens. The gift section is an unusual collection of items that Sheikh Zayed received during his lifetime, including golden swords and a golden palm tree. Al Ain is home to the last camel market of its kind in the UAE, located in with the livestock souk near Bawadi Mall. It is fascinating to stop and witness the traders discussing the merits and value of each animal. Traders

Off-Road UAE

The best way to check out the UAE's wonderfully contrasting landscapes is by 4WD. If you're an outdoors type, get your hands on the best-selling *UAE Off-Road Explorer*, which has 26 exciting off-road routes through desert, mountains and wadis, as well as info on places to see along the way.

are generally very friendly to tourists and you'll be able to get some great pictures, but remember to ask permission before clicking.

Buraimi is part of the Sultanate of Oman and you have to pass a border checkpoint to get there. Border crossing shouldn't take long, however, and a visit to the Omani side allows you to experience another culture. Buraimi Souk buzzes with local colour and atmosphere, and you'll find shops selling pottery, silver jewellery and woven carpets. Al Hili Fort, behind the souk, is a good starting point for exploring the Buraimi Oasis. Al Khandaq Fort, meanwhile, is thought to be around 400 years old and offers amazing views from its battlements.

Al Ain Hotels

Al Ain Rotana	03 754 5111
Al Massa Hotel	03 763 9003
Asfar Resorts	03 762 8882
Ayla Hotel	03 761 0111
City Seasons Hotel	03 755 0220
Danat Al Ain Resort	03 704 6000
Hilton Al Ain	03 768 6666
Mercure Grand Jebel Hafeet	03 783 8888

Al Ain Camel & Livestock Souk

Nr Bawadi Mall, Zayed Bin Sultan St abudhabi.ae

Conditions have improved dramatically with spacious pens for the animals and parking for visitors. A morning visit to the market is a fantastic way to mingle with locals and experience camel and goat trading as it has been for centuries. **Map** 4 H9

Al Ain National Museum

03 764 1595

Nr Sultan Fort, Zayed Bin Sultan St

abudhabi.ae

This museum, located on the edge of the main Al Ain Oasis, has a small but fascinating exhibit on the archaeology of the area, the culture and heritage of the people, and a selection of gifts received by Sheikh Zayed during his lifetime. There's also an interesting photography exhibition. **Map** 4 G8

Al Ain Oasis

03 712 8429

Zayed Bin Sultan St

abudhabi.ae

The area is divided into palm plantations, many of which are working farms. Visit this cool, tranquil area to see the ancient falaj system of irrigation, which draws water from underground. Other oases include the Al Gattara Oasis which has a heritage village. **Map** 4 G8

Al Ain Zoo

03 799 2000

Public Institution Zoo & Aquarium, Nahyan Al Awwal St

alainzoo.ae

Stretching over 900 hectares, this is one of the largest and best zoos in the Gulf. With ample greenery, a casual stroll through the park makes for a wonderful family day out. As well as seeing large mammals, reptiles, birds and big cats, you can get up close to some rare and common local species such as the Arabian oryx and sand gazelle. Since its founding, the zoo has been a centre for endangered species' conservation and visitors can spot true rarities. The park is home to a pair of white lions and tigers. A park train regularly departs from the central concourse, providing a whirlwind tour of the zoo. Opening times vary throughout the year, check the website. **Map** 4 G9

Al Jahili Fort & Park

03 784 3996

Nr Central Public Gardens

abudhabi.ae

One of the UAE's largest forts, the impressive Al Jahili Fort is over 100 years old and recently underwent extensive renovation. Now a cultural centre, it hosts large concerts as part of the Abu Dhabi Classics series as well as one off events and exhibitions. It is home to a permanent exhibition on British explorer, Wilfred Thesiger and his 1940s crossings of the Rub Al Khali desert. Opening hours, daily from 09:00-17:00, Friday from 15:00-17:00, closed on Mondays. **Map** 4 G8

Green Mubazzarah Park

03 783 9555

Nr Jebel Hafeet

At the base of the imposing Jebel Hafeet mountain are the natural springs of Green Mubazzarah. They are a grand spot to rest and paddle in the supposedly curative waters. Chalets are available should you wish to stay overnight. **Map** 4 G9

Hili Archaeological Gardens

Nr Dubai Highway, Mohammed Bin Khalifa St

abudhabi.ae

The gardens include an archaeological site and public spaces. There are remnants from a Bronze Age settlement, excavated and restored in 1995, and a number of the artefacts found are on display at the National Museum. **Map** 4 G7

Hili Fun City

Mohd Bin Khalifa St — 03 784 5542 — hilifuncity.ae

This 22-hectare theme park has recently been renovated to feature a number of new rides, while the leafy grounds provide an ideal spot for family picnics. Entrance costs from Dhs.35 and the park is open daily, except for during Ramadan when the facility closes for maintenance. **Map** 4 G7

Wadi Adventure

Nr Green Mubazzarah, Off Al Ain Fayda Rd — 03 781 8422 — wadiadventure.ae

A water park with a difference. Instead of slides, you'll find three white water rafting and kayaking runs, of more than a kilometre in length. A giant conveyor belt drags you to the summit and then it's up to you to complete the course. Beginner rapids are suitable for families. Surfers can also get in on the action with a huge pool that generates 3m high waves. Lessons are available. If water isn't your thing, tree-top obstacles and canyon swings should keep you occupied. Entrance is Dhs.100 for adults and Dhs.50 for children, activities are charged separately.
Map UAE Overview Map

Jebel Hafeet

Rising abruptly from the surrounding countryside, Jebel Hafeet dominates the area and the views from the top are simply unmissable. On a clear day you can see the surrounding desert plains, oases, wadis and the Hajar Mountain range in the distance. The road to the top is in excellent condition with a number of strategic viewpoints along the way.

Clockwise from top left: Al Jahili Fort, Al Ain Oasis, Al Ain National Museum

If you only do one thing in... Al Ain

Enjoy the lush greenery of the oasis.

Best for...

Eating & Drinking: Pop into the Mercure Grand Hotel for lunch on the terrace, or enjoy traditional Arabic food and entertainment in Min Zaman (03 754 5111) at the Al Ain Rotana (p.128).

Families: Spend the day getting acquainted with creatures big and small at Al Ain Zoo (p.129) or getting adventurous at Wadi Adventure (p.131).

Relaxation: Enjoy a dreamy few moments surrounded by palm trees in the tranquil shade of the Al Ain Oasis. Watch the ancient falaj irrigation system in action at the palm plantations.

Shopping: Witness haggling at its very best at the Livestock Souk (p.128).

Sightseeing: Swot up on the city's unique archaeology and history in the Al Ain Museum. Drive up Jebel Hafeet to enjoy spectacular views from the 1,180m summit.

Al Gharbia

With crystal clear seas and towering sand dunes, this undeveloped region to the west of the capital offers some of the UAE's most spectacular scenery.

Located to the west of Abu Dhabi, Al Gharbia makes up over two thirds of the UAE. Along its hundreds of kilometres of coastline can be found some stunning beaches, as well as a number of islands, which are increasingly being developed and promoted to visitors as high-end travel destinations. One of Al Gharbia's biggest attractions lies deep in the region's interior; Liwa is a mind-blowing destination with massive expanses of awesome desert and the biggest dunes this side of the Sahara. Whether you decide to rough it on a camping trip or stay in a luxury resort, you're guaranteed an unforgettable trip.

Desert Islands

02 406 1400

Off Jebel Dhanna, Sir Bani Yas Island, Al Gharbia, West of Abu Dhabi

desertislands.com

The eight desert islands are located off the Abu Dhabi coast near Jebel Dhanna. They are serviced by a ferry from the jetty at Marsa Jebel Dhanna and by two weekly flights to Sir Bani Yas Island from Abu Dhabi. Sir Bani Yas Island was originally created as a private wildlife sanctuary by the late Sheikh Zayed. Now it is a luxurious island resort and home to the Arabian Wildlife Park's 160 species of animals, which include cheetahs, hyenas, Arabian oryx and giraffe. The Desert

Islands Resort & Spa by Anantara (p.77) provides a luxurious base from which you can go hiking, mountain biking and kayaking, and get up close to the wildlife on a 4WD game safari. Alternatively, guests staying at the Danat Resort Jebel Dhanna can book a three-hour tour of the wildlife park.

Dalma Island has been inhabited for over 7,000 years and was once one of the most important centres of pearl fishing in the Gulf. Its history is captured in Dalma Museum and the various heritage buildings which have been restored on the island. The island is surprisingly verdant and can be visited via the ferry service from Marsa Jebel Dhanna on the mainland. The six Discovery Islands are still under development and closed to the public. Eventually they will provide luxurious eco-resort style accommodation along the lines of the Maldives.

Jebel Dhanna

230km west of Abu Dhabi

Located two hours west of Abu Dhabi, Jebel Dhanna is a great coastal getaway from the city. There are two hotels. The plush five-star resort Danat Jebel Dhanna Resort (danathotels.com) boasts stunning coastal views from the elegantly appointed rooms and suites, as well as half a mile of gorgeous white sand beaches for guests' use.

A Trip Of A Lifetime

To really experience Al Gharbia you need to ditch civilization and take on the desert wilderness. For help planning a Liwa trip, check out the *UAE Off-Road Explorer*, or contact a tour operator or the Western Region Development Council.

The lower rated Dhafra Beach Hotel (danathotels.com) provides landscaped gardens and a relaxed beachfront setting by the shallow turquoise waters of the Arabian Gulf.

Liwa

225km south of Abu Dhabi city

Prepare yourself for the most adventurous off-road driving the UAE has to offer, and some of its most incredible scenery; a trip to Liwa on the edge of the Empty Quarter (or Rub Al Khali) is a must for any off-roader during their time in the Middle East. Stretching into Oman, Yemen and Saudi Arabia, the Empty Quarter is the biggest sand desert on the planet, and the sheer scale of the scenery and the size of the dunes, which rise to heights of over 300m, has to be seen to be believed.

The Liwa area is home to one of the largest oases on the Arabian Peninsula which stretches over 150 kilometres and provides a surprising amount of greenery. While the main feature of Liwa is the desert, there are also several other attractions which are worth exploring along the way including tiny villages, a fish farm and some recently renovated forts. They are all interesting places to poke around in for an idea of the life that used to be in this remote corner of the country.

In order to access the biggest dunes and witness spectacular sunrises, camping is the most practical accommodation option. However, if home comforts are a necessity, try the convenient Liwa Hotel (almafrapearlhotels.com) which sits on the edge of the desert. Alternatively, the five-star Qasr Al Sarab Desert Resort by Anantara (p.77) on the edge of the Liwa crescent has all you need to make your wilderness experience a little more civilised.

Off-roading in Liwa

If you only do one thing in...
Al Gharbia

Get out into the desert – whether on a tour company day trip or a long weekend camping, the sheer scale of the sand dunes have to be seen to be believed.

Best for...

Families: Combine a luxurious night at the five-star Desert Islands Resort & Spa by Anantara (p.77) with an exciting 4WD safari of the Arabian Wildlife Park, spotting giraffe, hyenas and cheetahs.

Relaxing: Take time out in the deliciously chilled lagoon pool at Qasr Al Sarab (p.77). Break your sun bathing with a spa treatment, then sit back and watch the sun go down over the gorgeous dunes.

Sightseeing: Take a few days to experience the full Al Gharbia landscape. Spend a day travelling the coast road and explore Ras Kumais at the tip of the final peninsula before the Saudi border, where you'll find excellent seaside camping spots and crystal waters. Then head inland to tackle 300m tall sand dunes in Liwa, cross salt flats, explore the oasis and camp under the stars. Stop at the Emirates National Auto Museum on the way back.

Top: Qasr al Sarab; Bottom: 'ships of the desert'

Off The Beaten Track

From traditional sports to mountain safaris, there are plenty of reasons to leave your sun lounger and discover the wonders of this diverse country.

Abu Dhabi Pottery

02 666 7079

Nr Khalidiya Garden, 16th Street, Shk Zayed The First St, Al Khalidiyah

abudhabipottery.com

Excellent classes are available for adults, giving you the chance to try hand building and the wheel technique. There are also special kids' courses on offer for children aged over five. All classes cost Dhs.185 for adults and Dhs.100 for children, with supportive, knowledgeable instructors helping you create something original to take home. **Map** 3 C3

Al Maqam Camel Race Track

45km from Abu Dhabi, Al Ain Rd

Despite their ungainly appearance, camels can reach surprisingly high speeds and a trip to watch them race is highly recommended if you're in town during racing season. Al Maqam is the closest racetrack to the capital and race meetings are held on Friday and Saturday mornings between October and March, from around 07:30.

Freediving UAE

050 413 0486

Various Locations

freedivinguae.com

Step away from the scuba gear and try something a little different by diving in the way that nature intended. Abu

Dhabi-based Freediving UAE runs introductory and advanced AIDA courses, as well as regular training trips, so you can safely experience the incredible marine life of the Arabian Gulf (and even farther afield) without being hampered by the gear. Freedivinguae.com is also a great place to get hold of gear such as fins, masks and nose clips from brands such as Mares and Beuchat.

Noukhada Adventure Company — 02 558 1889

Bagala Supermarket Bldg, Khalifa City — noukhada.ae

The eastern side of Abu Dhabi island is flanked by a gorgeous mangrove forest which can only be properly explored by kayak, and eco-tour company Noukhada runs serene two-hour tours through the mangroves, focusing on the unique eco-system. Tours cost just Dhs.150 per person, including equipment rental. Longer trips (along with overnight stays on local islands, full moon night tours and kayak fishing) are also available.

Women's Handicraft Centre — 02 447 6645

Women's Association Complex, Al Karama St, Al Mushrif

This government-supported centre consists of a series of huts in which local women practise traditional crafts, such as weaving, silver threading and, perhaps most popularly with tourists, henna body art. It's perfect for picking up some traditional mementos but be careful to photograph only the products and not the women themselves. There's also a nice cafe on the premises, where you can sample traditional Arabic fare. **Map** 1 C3

Further Out

Beyond the capital, the UAE has spectacular sights and experiences, from bustling cities of man-made wonders to mountain pools and desert retreats.

The six other emirates which make up the UAE lie to the north of Abu Dhabi and only occupy 13% of the country's landmass. Dubai, Sharjah, Ajman, Umm Al Quwain, and Ras Al Khaimah lie on the west coast, and Fujairah on the east coast. Each of the emirates has its own distinct character: Dubai is a glitzy tourist hotspot, Sharjah is the undisputed culture capital, and Fujairah is home to breathtakingly beautiful landscapes. If your stay in Abu Dhabi is long enough to permit exploration of the other emirates, you should definitely make the effort to experience their unique characteristics.

Dubai

Located an hour and a half away from Abu Dhabi by car, Dubai is a fascinating city to visit. Among the high-rises you'll find the tallest building in the world, the Burj Khalifa (burjkhalifa.ae), a selection of the world's most luxurious hotels, some amazing leisure facilities (an indoor ski slope with real snow, to name just one), opulent designer hotels, celebrity-chef endorsed restaurants, and several stunning beaches. There are also a number of world renowned events worth checking out, including the Emirates Rugby Sevens (December), the Dubai Tennis Championships (February),

Burj Khalifa & Downtown Dubai

the Dubai World Cup horse race (March) and golf's Dubai Desert Classic (February) and Dubai World Championship (November). Dubai's reputation as a progressive place is not undeserved, and it's a great destination for a night out; whether you're after a slap up meal in a five-star hotel, a cheap Indian curry, sundowners at a casual beach bar, or dancing till the early hours at an exclusive nightclub, Dubai's entertainment scene will not disappoint.

Renowned as the 'shopping capital of the Middle East', Dubai is the ultimate place for a shopaholic with a healthy credit limit. The enormous Ibn Battuta Mall, Mall of the Emirates (the one with the ski slope) and the record-breaking Dubai Mall are all easily accessible from the highway, or you could go bargain hunting at the Outlet Mall.

Just be aware that the drive from Abu Dhabi can be pretty hair-raising. Defensive driving is not an option – it's essential.

East Coast

Even if you're only in the UAE for a short time, a trip to the East Coast is a must. You can get there in two to three hours from Abu Dhabi.

The diving is considered better than that of the west coast, mainly because of increased visibility. Snoopy Island and Dibba Rock are among the favourite spots for diving and snorkelling. The East Coast is also home to a few other sights, many of which are free to explore. The site of the oldest mosque in the UAE, Badiyah, is roughly half way down the East Coast, north of Khor Fakkan. The building is believed to date back to the middle of the 15th century and was restored in 2003. The village is considered one of the oldest settlements on the East Coast, and is thought to have been inhabited since 3000BC. Located at the northernmost point of the East Coast, Dibba is made up of three fishing villages, each coming under a different jurisdiction: Sharjah, Fujairah, and Oman. The villages share an attractive bay and excellent diving locations. The Hajar Mountains provide a wonderful backdrop to the public beaches. Further north, across the border into Oman, is Khasab, a great base for exploring the inlets and unspoilt waters of Musandam. You can stay at the Golden Tulip (goldentulipkhasab.com), which can organise dhow cruises and dolphin watching, both of which are recommended, or the luxurious Six Senses Hideaway Zighy Bay (sixsenses.com).

Further south on the coast lies Fujairah, the youngest of the seven emirates. Overlooking the atmospheric old town is a fort that is reportedly about 300 years old. The surrounding hillsides are dotted with more ancient forts and watchtowers, which add an air of mystery and charm. Abu Dhabi residents often use Fujairah as a base for exploring the rest of the coast. Hotels include Le Meridien Al Aqah (lemeridien-alaqah.com), and Radisson Blu Fujairah (radissonblu.com).

Khor Kalba sits just south of Fujairah and is the most northerly mangrove forest in the world, and home to varieties of plant, marine and bird life not found anywhere else in the UAE. A canoe tour by Desert Rangers (p.152) is the best way to reach the heart of the mangrove reserve.

Hatta

Hatta is a small town, nestled at the food of the Hajar Mountains, about 100km from Dubai city and 10km from the Dubai-Oman border. The road leading to Hatta from Dubai (E44) is a trip in itself. Watch as the sand gradually changes from beige to dark orange and then disappears, only to be replaced by jagged mountains. The famous Big Red sand dune lies off this road, and is a popular spot for dune driving in 4WDs or quad bikes. You'll also pass a row of carpet shops, ideal for putting your bargaining skills into practice.

Hatta is home to the oldest fort in Dubai emirate, which was built in 1790. You'll also see several watchtowers on the surrounding hills. The town itself has a sleepy, relaxed feel, and includes the Heritage Village (04 852 1374), which charts the area's 3,000 year history and includes a 200 year old mosque, and the fortress built by Sheikh Maktoum bin Hasher Al Maktoum in 1896, which is now used as a weaponry museum. The Hatta Fort Hotel (jebelali-international.com) offers bungalow-style luxury rooms and sports and leisure facilities including shooting and mini-golf.

In the mountains beyond the village are the Hatta Pools, where you can see deep, strangely shaped canyons carved out by rushing floodwater. The trail towards the pools is graded, so a two-wheel drive car and some skilled driving should be enough to get you there. From the Dubai-Hatta road, take a right at the fort roundabout, then a left towards the Heritage Village, another left at the roundabout, and then the first main right. Drive through a second village; where the tarmac ends take the gravel track on your right. For tours see p.150.

Northern Emirates

North of Dubai are Sharjah, Ajman, Umm Al Quwain and Ras Al Khaimah. These emirates are smaller in size than Dubai and Abu Dhabi and are also less developed.

Ajman is the smallest of the emirates, but its proximity to Dubai and Sharjah has enabled it to grow considerably. It has one of the largest dhow building centres in the region, offering a chance to see these massive wooden boats being built with rudimentary tools using skills passed down through the generations. Ajman also has some great beaches and a pleasant corniche. Much of the nightlife revolves around the Ajman Kempinski Hotel & Resort (kempinski.com).

Umm Al Quwain has the smallest population and little has changed over the years. It is home to the expansive Dreamland Aqua Park (dreamlanduae.com). Two of the most interesting activities Umm Al Quwain has to offer are crab hunting and mangrove tours; the Flamingo Beach Resort (flamingoresort.ae) offers both.

Ras Al Khaimah is the most northerly of the seven emirates but you can make the trip from Abu Dhabi in around three hours. With the jagged Hajar Mountains rising just behind the city, and the Arabian Gulf stretching out from the shore, RAK has some of the best scenery in the UAE. A creek divides the city into the old town and the newer Al Nakheel district. For a day trip, you should go to the souk in the old town and the National Museum of Ras Al Khaimah (07 233 3411). From there you can explore the surrounding countryside and visit the ancient sites of Ghalilah and Shimal.

Sharjah

Before Dubai's rise to prominence as a trading and tourism hotspot in this part of the country, neighbouring Sharjah was one of the wealthiest towns in the region, with settlers earning their livelihood from fishing, pearling and trade. Sharjah is worth a visit for its various museums and great shopping. Its commitment to art, culture and preserving its traditional heritage is well known throughout the Arab world. Sharjah is built around Khalid Lagoon (popularly known as the creek), and the surrounding Buheirah Corniche is a popular spot for an evening stroll. From various points on the lagoon, small dhows can be hired to see the lights of the city from the water. The Heritage Area (sharjahtourism.ae) is a fascinating old walled city, home to numerous museums and the traditional Souk Al Arsah. The nearby Arts Area is a treat for art lovers with galleries and more museums. A must is Al Qasba (qaq.ae), one of Sharjah's top attractions with performance spaces and waterside restaurants. Another worthy stop-off is the Sharjah Natural History Museum (sharjahmuseums.ae). Shoppers shouldn't miss the beautiful Central Souk, also known as the Blue Souk. The two buildings contain more than 600 shops selling gold and knick-knacks. This is one of the best places in the UAE to buy carpets.

Oman

Just a few hours from Abu Dhabi, you'll find the countless attractions of Oman. It's a breathtakingly scenic country, with history and culture to boot. The capital, Muscat, has enough attractions to keep you busy for a short break,

Musandam

including beautiful beaches, some great restaurants and cafes, and the mesmerising old souk at Mutrah. Out of the capital you will find many historic old towns and forts, and some of the most stunning mountain and wadi scenery in the region. Salalah, in the south, has the added bonus of being cool and wet in the summer. Isolated from the rest of the country, on the tip of the Arabian Peninsula, is the Omani enclave of Musandam. With its jagged mountains and fjord-like inlets, it has the moniker 'the Norway of the Middle East' and is a must-visit if you are in Abu Dhabi for any serious length of time. A flight from Abu Dhabi to Muscat takes less than an hour and daily flights are operated by Etihad, Gulf Air and Oman Air. There is also a bus service from Abu Dhabi to both Muscat and Salalah. For further information see the *Oman Guide*.

Tours & Sightseeing

Whether by boat, bus or 4WD, an organised tour is a hassle-free way of maximising your sightseeing time and experiencing a different side to the UAE.

An organised tour can be a great way of discovering the Emirates, especially if you're only here for a short time. Whether you prefer activities, sightseeing or shopping, you'll find a tour to suit you. The majority of tours need to be booked in advance and most tour operators visit the main hotels in order to book tours for guests. Some trips may need to be arranged further in advance, especially if they involve travel to another emirate. Hotel concierges should have information on which tours are available and when and may even be able to get you a special deal.

Almost all tour operators offer the usual tours: city tours, desert safaris and mountain safaris. Some, however, offer more unique activities, such as fishing or diving trips, trips to see the Empty Quarter in Liwa, shopping tours and desert driving courses. Contact the companies on p.152 for some ideas. If they don't have exactly what you want, they're sure to know someone who does.

Big Bus Tours

Tour Abu Dhabi city on the top floor of a double decker bus, hopping on and off as you please and learning some fascinating facts en route. Find out more at bigbustours.com.

Tours & Sightseeing

Absolute Adventure	04 345 9900	adventure.ae
Abu Dhabi Travel Bureau	02 6338 700	abudhabitravelbureau.com
Advanced Travel & Tourism	02 634 7900	advancedtravels.net
Al Ain Golden Sands Tourism	03 768 8006	alaings.com
Al Badeyah Eyes Tourism	02 445 2644	abet-uae.com
Al Badie Travel Agency	02 632 2775	albadietravel.com
Al Masood Travel & Services	02 652 1800	almasaoodtravel.com
Arabian Adventures	02 691 1711	arabian-adventures.com
Cyclone Travel & Tours	02 627 6275	cyclonetours.com
Desert Adventures Tourism	02 556 6155	desertadventures.com
Desert Rangers	04 357 2200	desertrangers.com
Emirates Tours & Safari	02 491 2929	eatours.ae
Hala Abu Dhabi	02 617 7811	halaabudhabi.ae
Kurban Tours	02 555 0566	kurbantours.com
Net Tours	02 679 4658	nettoursuae.ae
Orient Tours	02 667 5609	orienttours.ae
Safar Travel & Tourism	02 418 0888	safar.ae
Salem Travel Agency	02 621 8000	salemtravelagency.com
Sunshine Tours	02 444 9914	adnh.com

Sports & Spas

Active Abu Dhabi	156
Sports & Activities	158
Spectator Sports	172
Out Of Abu Dhabi	176
Spas	178

103

Active Abu Dhabi

Best known as a sun-soaked luxury destination, Abu Dhabi offers much more – from golf and diving to a spot of relaxation at one of the spas.

Visitors to Abu Dhabi are sure to be delighted by the wide variety of sports and activities available, from the wonderfully indulgent to the adrenaline-fuelled. Winter (October to March) is the best time to enjoy outdoor activities (although many visitors take part in such pursuits all year round), whether it's mainstream sports like golf and tennis or alternative options such as caving, mountain biking, rock climbing and skydiving. For those less keen on the summer heat, there are plenty of indoor activities available, and most hotels have excellent gym facilities.

During the hotter months, early mornings and late evenings are the best options for outdoor activities, be it watersports, a round of floodlit golf, or a walk along the Corniche (p.90).

If you are interested in having a go at adventure activities such as climbing, off-roading, mountain biking, dune buggying or quad biking, then there are a number of reputable tour operators (see p.152) that offer tailored activity trips. Taking a trip out into the wilderness is a must, and there are various tours on offer (p.150). Places to see include the Rub Al Khali or 'Empty Quarter' (the last great frontier of uninhabited desert), the many oases hidden among the dunes or the dramatic wadis and jagged mountains rising out

Mountain biking

of the desert. If you've got the confidence (and the insurance) and are in a group you can hire a 4WD, pick up a copy of the *UAE Off-Road Explorer* or *UAE & Oman Ultimate Explorer*, and explore the unpaved expanses yourself.

Over the past few years, Abu Dhabi has made quite a name for itself on the international sporting scene. The Etihad Airways Abu Dhabi grand prix at Yas Marina Circuit (p.170) is now a fixture on the Formula 1 calendar, and the Abu Dhabi HSBC Golf Championship, which hosts several of the world's best golfers, is the curtain-raiser for the European PGA Tour. Tennis fans, meanwhile, get to witness some of the world's top players starting the new sporting year at the Mubadala World Tennis Championships (mubadalawtc.com).

Sports & Activities

Whether you're setting sail along the Corniche or teeing off on a world-class golf course, Abu Dhabi has much to offer the active visitor.

Dhow Charters & Cruises

Abu Dhabi's beautiful coastline makes taking a dhow charter or a coastal cruise an absolute must when in town.

Al Dhafra

02 673 2266

Nr Meena Fish Market, Al Meena

aldhafra.net

As well as dinner cruises, Al Dhafra has several traditional Arabian dhows available for charter. Trips can be arranged for fishing, sightseeing and private parties. Avid anglers are advised to take their own equipment as there is only a limited amount on board. Charters cost from Dhs.180 per person, or a dhow for 20 can be hired for Dhs.600 per hour. **Map** 3 G1

The Yellow Boats

800 8044

Marina Mall, Breakwater

theyellowboats.com

These high speed boat tours are not for the faint of heart. The 30 minute rides where the skipper shows off the boat's abilities cost Dhs.150; there's a 30 minute Emirates Palace and Corniche tour available for the same price; while the 50 minute tour covers the Corniche and Lulu Island for Dhs.200. The boats can also be chartered by the hour or hired for corporate events. **Map** 3 B1.

Golf

Abu Dhabi is rapidly making its mark as a leading international golf destination. Global television coverage of the Abu Dhabi HSBC Golf Championship, a European PGA tour event attracting some of the leading names in international golf, is dramatically raising the emirate's profile among the world's golf enthusiasts and, with some amazing courses to choose from, it's easy to see why. You can even play on an all sand, or 'brown' golf course.

Abu Dhabi City Golf Club

02 445 9600
Saeed Bin Tahnoon St, Al Mushrif
adcitygolf.ae

This par 70 course boasts one of the longest par five holes in the Gulf, at 630 yards. Although there are only nine holes, there are alternate tees for the back nine. Green fees for visitors start at Dhs.270 for 18 holes and Dhs.145 for nine holes with cart hire. Range balls cost Dhs.40 per bucket for non-members and free for members. **Map** 2 H13

Abu Dhabi Golf Club

02 558 8990
Umm Al Nar St, Khalifa City
adgolfclub.com

Located 30 minutes from the city centre, this is the venue for the Abu Dhabi HSBC Golf Championship. The club's impressive offering includes the challenging 18 hole, 7,334 yard, par 72 Championship Course as well as the slightly more forgiving Garden Course. There are plenty of other facilities, including a golf institute, a 350 metre driving range, practice facilities, a clubhouse, pro-shop and pool, and a choice of food and drink options. **Map** 1 F4

Al Ain Golf Club
03 768 6808

Nr Danat Al Ain Resort, Al Ain

The Al Ain Golf Club, east of the Danat Al Ain Resort, boasts an 18 hole sand course and a floodlit driving range. Handicaps gained here are valid internationally. Visitors are welcome, but should phone ahead. The sand is treated and compacted, creating a smooth surface that putts similar to a green. **Map** 4 H8

Al Ghazal Golf Club
02 575 8040

Nr Abu Dhabi Intl Airport, Airport Area
alghazalgolf.ae

This purpose-built 18 hole sand golf course, driving range, academy and licensed clubhouse is situated just a couple of minutes from the capital's airport, and the club has hosted the Abu Dhabi World Sand Golf Championship. No reservations are usually required and anyone can play here, including transit passengers with a few hours to kill – airlines can arrange 96-hour passenger transit visas for travellers who want to play golf or use the facilities. **Map** 1 J4

Hilton Al Ain Golf Club
03 768 6666

Hilton Al Ain, Al Ain
al-ain.hilton.com

The holes of this par three chip and putt course may only average about 80 yards in length but, although short, it can be a tough golfing test. The course has nearly 30 bunkers and very small, quick greens. It is open to non-members, and lessons are available to book. There is an entrance fee of Dhs.23 for non-members and club hire starts from Dhs.35 for a half set. **Map** 4 H8

Saadiyat Beach Golf Club

Saadiyat Island — 02 557 8000 — sbgolfclub.ae

The 18 hole course at Saadiyat Beach Golf Club was designed by Gary Player. In addition to its beautiful setting, the course should provide enough challenge to even the most passionate of golfers. For the less experienced, the Golf Institute by Troon Golf offers the chance to perfect your swing with an introduction to the golf course and a junior development programme. **Map** 1 D1

Yas Links Abu Dhabi

Nr Yas Marina Circuit, Yas Island West — 02 810 7777 — yaslinks.com

Designed by Kyle Phillips, Yas Links is one of the region's top golf destinations. It boasts an 18 hole course in a stunningly scenic setting as part of the Yas Island development, with gorgeous seashore views. Open since 2010, there's also a nine hole academy course, clubhouse, golf academy and floodlit practice facilities. Rack rates start at Dhs.550 for non-members. **Map** 1 H3

Wadi & Dune Bashing

Bouncing over the dunes in a buggy is exhilarating, addictive, and definitely one of the best ways to experience the desert. A popular location for dune buggies and quad bike riders is behind Al Ain airport, where locals and expats go to take advantage of the clean dunes and wide open spaces. Desert Rangers (desertrangers.com) offers dune buggy tours, where you can enjoy all the thrills and spills of this extreme sport in the safest possible way – the company provides training, all the safety equipment you'll need, and an experienced leader to guide you through the dunes. Alternatively, you can hire a quad bike from independent companies, most commonly found in the Big Red area on the road from Dubai to Hatta. A variety of quads are available on an hourly basis.

Most car rental agencies offer visitors 4WDs capable of desert driving. If renting a 4WD, make sure you get the details of the insurance plan, as many rental insurers won't cover damage caused by off-roading. Most major tour companies offer a range of desert and mountain safaris if you'd rather leave the driving to the professionals. Driving in wadis is usually a bit more straightforward. Wadis are (usually) dry gullies, carved through the rock by rushing floodwaters, following the course of seasonal rivers. When out in a wadi keep your eyes open for rare, but not impossible, thunder storms developing. The wadis can fill up quickly and you will need to make your way to higher ground pretty quickly to avoid flash floods. For further information and tips on off-road driving in the UAE, check out the *UAE Off-Road Explorer.*

Watersports & Diving

With an ideal climate and the warm waters of the Gulf on its doorstep, Abu Dhabi is a great location for watersports. The Beach Rotana Abu Dhabi (02 697 9000) in the Tourist Club area offers several options, including waterskiing, wakeboarding and windsurfing, with Dubai's successful Watercooled (watercooleddubai.com) also opening up a beach house at the Hilton Abu Dhabi, from where every watersport imaginable is available. Outside Abu Dhabi island, Al Raha Beach Hotel (p.67) rents jetskis, as does Jet Ski Ghantoot (jetskidubai.com).

Snorkelling equipment is available for hire at most hotels or dive centres. Most hotels contract out their watersports operations, so be sure the company you deal with has full insurance and that the equipment is in good order. Kitesurfing has taken off in the emirate and there are several instructors with whom you can set up a two or three-hour lesson that includes equipment rental. For a listing of Abu Dhabi-based kitesurfing instructors, visit ad-kitesurfing.net.

The waters around the UAE are rich in a variety of marine and coral life as well as several submerged wrecks. Most dive companies also organise trips to Musandam, the spectacular Omani enclave north of the UAE. For further information on diving in the region, refer to the *UAE Underwater Explorer* or the *UAE & Oman Ultimate Explorer*.

7 Seas Divers

09 238 7400

Nr Safeer Centre, Al Mudifi, Khor Fakkan — 7seasdivers.com

This PADI dive centre offers day and night diving trips to sites around Khor Fakkan, Musandam and Lima Rock. Training is provided from beginner to instructor level, in several different languages.

Abu Dhabi Sub Aqua Club

02 673 1111

The Club, Mina Zayed Free Port — the-club.com

This club is affiliated to the British Sub Aqua Club (BSAC), so you can rest assured that the safety standards are high. The club regularly organises training courses for all levels and standards, including absolute beginners. Dive trips are at weekends and include locations around Abu Dhabi, Musandam and Khor Fakkan on the east coast, where the club rents a villa. Membership is only open to members of The Club (p.103). For more information see the website. **Map** 1 C2

Al Forsan International Sports Resort
02 556 8555
Nr Abu Dhabi Golf Club & Resort, Khalifa City
alforsan.com

Al Forsan is a world-class cable boarding facility. The main difference between cable boarding and normal wakeboarding (or waterskiing) is that there is no need for a boat. Instead, the strong cable links wired around the lakes pull you along. Many find cable boarding the ideal way to start boarding thanks to the calm waters and steady tension on the tow line; one of the lakes at Al Forsan is dedicated entirely to beginners. Over on the expert lake, boarders and skiers zip their way around, jumping over ramps while practising surface switches. Equipment, including the mandatory life jacket and helmets, are provided and staff are on hand with helpful tips. Prices range from Dhs.125 for an hour to Dhs.280 for the day. **Map** 1 G4

Arabian Divers & Sportfishing Charters > *p.165*
050 614 6931
Nr UAE Central Bank, Marina Al Bateen Resort, Al Bateen
fishabudhabi.com

This well-established tour operator offers a range of scuba diving experiences, as well as big game fishing in the Gulf and

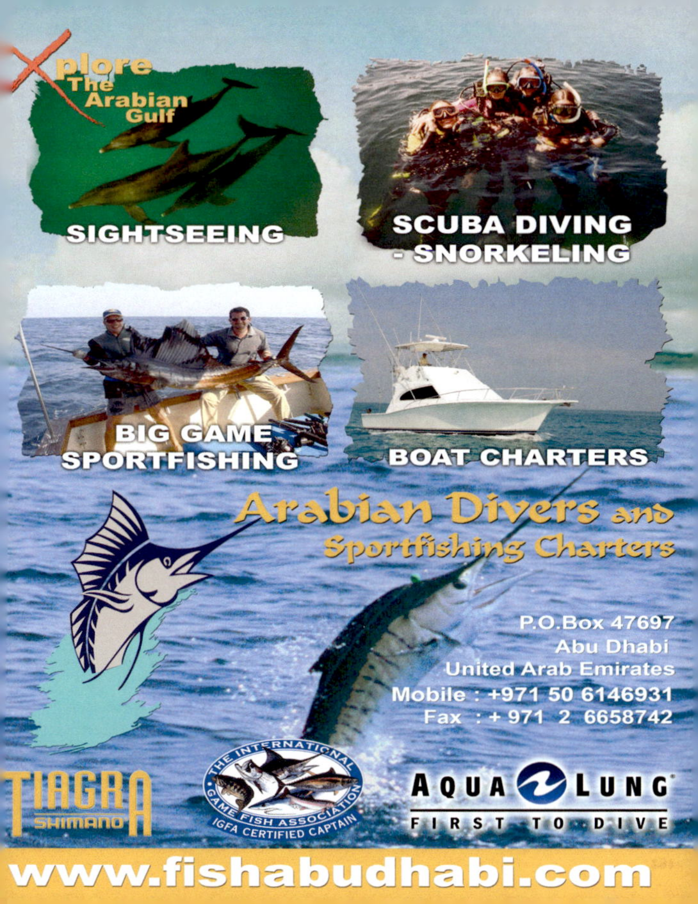
Xplore The Arabian Gulf
SIGHTSEEING
SCUBA DIVING - SNORKELING
BIG GAME SPORTFISHING
BOAT CHARTERS
Arabian Divers and Sportfishing Charters
P.O.Box 47697
Abu Dhabi
United Arab Emirates
Mobile : +971 50 6146931
Fax : + 971 2 6658742
TIAGRA SHIMANO
THE INTERNATIONAL GAME FISH ASSOCIATION
IGFA CERTIFIED CAPTAIN
AQUA LUNG
FIRST TO DIVE
www.fishabudhabi.com

boat charters. You'll find all the on-site facilities you need at its Al Bateen Marina location including a shop, a classroom and a training pool. The company is renowned for offering individual attention and keeping diving groups small, making sure that safety comes first. PADI courses from beginner to advanced are available. **Map** 3C4

Sandy Beach Diving Centre

09 244 5555
Sandy Beach Hotel & Resort, Fujairah
sandybm.com

Located over on the east coast, this is one of the UAE's oldest and best-known dive centres – you can stay at the Sandy Beach Hotel too and enjoy several days of diving. The centre offers a qualified team of instructors and support staff. Its famous house reef, Snoopy Island, is alive with marine life and is excellent for snorkelling and diving. Trips to Dibba, Khor Fakkan and Musandam are also offered.
Map UAE Overview Map

Wadi Adventure

03 781 8422
Nr Green Mubazzarah, Off Al Ain Fayda Rd, Al Ain
wadiadventure.ae

The Al Ain desert might be the last place you'd expect to find a whole host of watersports, but Wadi Adventure is the only man-made facility of its kind in the Middle East, offering white water rafting and kayaking runs, as well as guaranteed 3m high breaks for surfers in the giant wave pool. There are also a few food and drink outlets for refuelling. Entrance for adults is Dhs.100, Dhs.50 for children below 1.2m, with each activity then charged separately. **Map** UAE Overview Map

Yas Waterworld
02 414 2000
Yas Island
yaswaterworld.com

As well as the slides, rollercoaster, pools, lazy river and suspended rollercoaster, Yas Waterworld has a couple of 'waveriders' – basically, simulated surf swells that surfer dudes in need of artificial waves can use for bodyboarding. While first-timers will be happy just to stay on for their allotted time, more experienced riders can learn to pull all sorts of spins and tricks. There are, of course, plenty of food and drink stands around if you work up a hunger or a thirst. **Map** 1 H3

Motorsports

The UAE deserts provide ideal locations for rallying, and many events are organised throughout the year by the Emirates Motor Sports Federation (EMSF). In addition to the Abu Dhabi Desert Classic, the other events include the Spring Desert Rally (4WD), Peace Rally (saloons), Jeep Jamboree (safari), Drakkar Noir 1000 Dunes Rally (4WD), Shell Festival Parade, Audi Driving Skills (driving challenge) and Federation Rally (4WD). For details, call EMSF (04 282 7111) or visit the website (emsf.ae). Closer to the city, Ferrari World, Yas Marina Circuit and Al Forsan provide petrol-fuelled thrills and activities, including go-karting.

Al Forsan International Sports Resort
02 556 8555
Nr Abu Dhabi Golf Club & Resort, Khalifa City
alforsan.com

Al Forsan has an extensive and excellent Motor Sports Centre, which offers up a range of petrol-powered activities

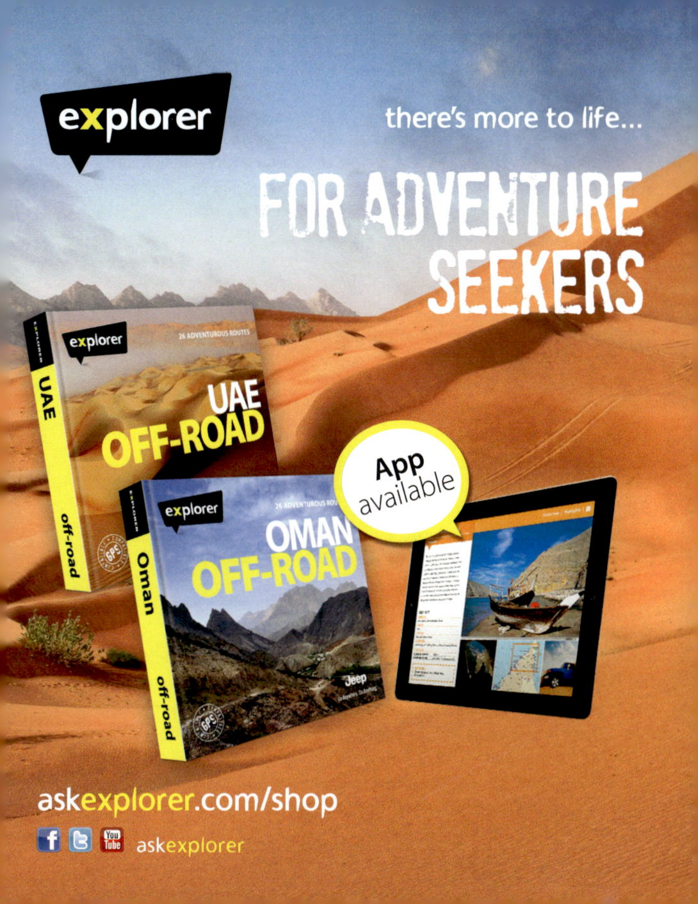
explorer
there's more to life...
FOR ADVENTURE SEEKERS
explorer
26 ADVENTUROUS ROUTES
UAE OFF-ROAD
UAE off-road
explorer
OMAN OFF-ROAD
Oman off-road
Jeep
App available
askexplorer.com/shop
askexplorer

for driving fans. There's the 1.2km CIK approved circuit with various possible layouts and vehicles with top speeds of up to 120kph available (only for experienced karters – slower karts are available for those who don't already drive like Fernando Alonso); there's also a less high-speed kids' karting track. The dual circuit fully-floodlit off-road buggy track allows two buggies to race without chance of collision, and there's also an alternative use circuit, where drivers can learn to master the arts of drifting, skid control and power turns. All facilities use state-of-the-art safety and timing equipment. **Map** 1 G5

Ferrari World Abu Dhabi

02 496 8001
Yas Island West
ferrariworldabudhabi.com

The world's largest indoor theme park has enough attractions to keep motorsports enthusiasts of all ages entertained. Kids can learn to drive in a miniature Ferrari, while grown-up fans get to take a glimpse into the F1 paddock or experience race driving in a simulator. For thrillseekers, there's the world's fastest rollercoaster, the Formula Rossa. **Map** 1 H3

Yas Marina Circuit

02 659 9800
Yas Island
yasmarinacircuit.com

While most famous as the home of the annual Formula 1 Etihad Airways grand prix, Yas Marina Circuit is a year-round venue where petrolheads can put their driving skills to the test, or take high-speed driving lessons. The long list of possibilities includes karting, drag racing, as well as a host of other options from supercar driving to passenger experiences. **Map** 1 H3

Clockwise from top: Formula 1 race car, Ferrari World, Yas Marina Circuit

vodafone

FERRARI WORLD

ALDAR
ALDAR

Spectator Sports

Abu Dhabi has an exciting line-up of events for sports enthusiasts; from golf to motorsports, there should be plenty on offer to keep you entertained.

A wide range of sporting events are organised in Abu Dhabi and the emirate is backing an increasing number of international events. The sunny climate, location within easy reach of Europe and Asia, and development of some excellent facilities mean the country is growing more attractive as a venue. Fans of live action can enjoy anything from motorsports at the Formula 1 Abu Dhabi GP (p.58) to powerboat racing (p.58) along the Corniche.

Camel Racing

This spectacular sport can be one of the most memorable highlights of any visit to the UAE. The traditional sport involves ungainly animals being ridden around a track by robots, since the use of young child jockeys was banned. It has developed into a professional sport in the UAE with Dhs.25 million to be won as prize money each year. Races normally take place on weekend mornings during winter, with additional races on National Day and public holidays. Try to be at the track early on a Friday morning to soak up the atmosphere. Al Wathba Camel Race track is about 45km east of Abu Dhabi, and Al Maqam track is near Al Ain. You will also have the opportunity to meet camel owners and can bargain for some camel racing paraphernalia such as blankets, rugs and beads, or even buy a camel – they cost anything from Dhs.2,000 to Dhs.15,000. Entrance to the races is free of charge for spectators.

Golf

Abu Dhabi HSBC Golf Championship

Abu Dhabi Golf Club,
Khalifa City abudhabigolfchampionship.com

With more than $2m in prize money and some of the biggest names in golf, the annual Abu Dhabi Golf Championship is the European PGA Tour curtain-raiser, held at the stunning Abu Dhabi Golf Club (p.114). Away from the action there are children's entertainment, competitions and food and beverage outlets, providing a fantastic family day out.

Map 1 F4

Horse Racing

Abu Dhabi Equestrian Club

02 445 5500
Shakhbout Bin Sultan St, Al Mushrif adec-web.com

If you are looking for something different on a Sunday evening, race night atmosphere is hard to beat. The season lasts from October to April. The six or seven races per meeting start every 30 minutes, from 18:00. Entry to the public area is free, as are the race cards. The Tri Cast Competition invites race goers to pick the first three finishers in each race. Entries must be submitted before the first race, and there are prizes for the winners. For further details, call 02 445 5500 or visit adec-web.com. Map 1 C4

Motorsports

The Formula 1 Etihad Airways Abu Dhabi grand prix (p.58) is a high-profile three-day sports and entertainment event. In addition to the high-octane F1 race, other racing events take place at the Yas Marina Circuit throughout the year. The Abu Dhabi Desert Challenge (abudhabidesertchallenge.com) is another popular event, in which motorbikes and 4WDs battle it out over the dunes.

Powerboat Racing

The Abu Dhabi Powerboat Championship is part of the 10 stage UIM F1 powerboat racing World Championship. The event is a joint programme by Abu Dhabi and Sharjah featuring individual championship and team events. At this December event, up to 24 boats representing 12 nations compete at high speed along the twisting course off the Corniche. For more information, go to f1h2o.com. The Abu Dhabi International Marine Sports Club organises the annual President's Cup F2000 Powerboat Championship, the National Regatta, the National Jet-ski Championship, and the UAE Wooden Powerboat Championship, all of which are designed to encourage young Emiratis to remain close to their marine heritage. Each season also sees two open regattas for modern boats (including catamarans, lasers and windsurfers), which are open to all ages and nationalities. ADIMSC also has a racing calendar, which runs from December to May.

Mubadala World Tennis Championship

Tennis

Mubadala World Tennis Championship

02 493 8888

Zayed Sports City, Al Safarat

mubadalawtc.com

Abu Dhabi's first international tennis championship was held in 2009 and top players, including Roger Federer and Rafael Nadal, have taken part each year since. The tournament has become very popular and you should buy tickets well in advance. The event features family attractions as well as a series of tennis-based activities and tournaments during the run-up to the event, including the Community Cup. The three-day event usually takes place just before or over New Year. **Map** 2 B2

Out Of Abu Dhabi

Although Abu Dhabi offers a plethora of ways to get active, head further afield and you'll find plenty more still.

DP World Tour Championship

Dubai europeantour.com

The Dubai World Championship is the grand finale of The Race to Dubai, the European Tour's season-long competition which features 46 tournaments in 24 destinations. This annual tournament runs for four days and is open to the leading 60 players in The Race to Dubai rankings after the 45th event, ensuring that the cream of the golf world qualify for the chance to compete for a prize fund of $8 million, with an additional $3.75 million bonus pool for the top 10 finishers.

Dubai Duty Free Tennis Championships

04 417 2415

Dubai Tennis Stadium, Dubai dubaidutyfreetennischampionships.com

The Dubai Tennis Championships takes place every February at the Aviation Club in Garhoud; it offers a great opportunity to catch some of the top players in the game at close quarters. The $2 million event is firmly established on the international tennis calendar, and features both men's and ladies' tournaments. Tickets for the finals sell out in advance, but entrance to the earlier rounds can be bought on the day.

Dubai World Cup

04 327 0077

Meydan Racecourse, Dubai

dubaiworldcup.com

The buzzing atmosphere at the richest horse race in the world makes it one of the year's big social occasions, and it all takes place in Meydan, the world's most state-of-the-art racing venue. Complete with fancy frocks and fireworks, the main event, held in late March, is an event not to be missed; otherwise, you can see a slightly more raw form of horse racing at Jebel Ali racecourse (04 347 4914), near The Greens.

Emirates Airlines Dubai Rugby Sevens

04 321 0008

The Sevens, Dubai

dubairugby7s.com

One of the biggest fixtures in the UAE, the Dubai Rugby Sevens is a three-day event which plays host to the top 16 Sevens teams in the world. The first day of the event sees regional teams go head to head with the international teams joining the fray for the last two days. As well as the main matches, you can also watch social, youth and women's games at the event. Tickets regularly sell out so plan early. The event takes place at a facility called 'The Sevens' on Al Ain Road.

Omega Dubai Desert Classic

04 380 2112

Emirates Golf Club, Dubai

dubaidesertclassic.com

One of the highlights of the Dubai sporting calendar, this European PGA Tour competition is a popular event among both players and spectators, held at the end of January and start of February. Top golfers who have previously competed in the event include Tiger Woods and Ernie Els.

Spas

Arabian luxury extends to splendid spas that will transport you to paradise. If you want to feel like Cleopatra then you've come to the right place.

No luxury holiday is complete without a trip to the spa for a truly hedonistic head-to-toe pampering session. Abu Dhabi is home to a host of excellent facilities, so whether you fancy a facial or desire a day of indulgence, you will find a wide variety of treatments on offer for the mind, body and face. From anti-ageing to body firming you will leave feeling like a new person, and the sheer luxury of many spas is an experience in its own right. Unique to the region is the traditional Arabian treatment, the luxurious hammam experience, involving a full-body henna mask and some serious scrubbing – definitely not one for the inhibited!

Anantara Spa

02 656 1146

Eastern Mangroves Hotel & Spa by Anantara
Al Matar

spa.anantara.com

Levels of luxury cannot be faulted here, with 10 self-contained treatment rooms (two of which can be used by couples) as well as a stunning hammam, sauna and steam rooms, all offering Thai relaxation with Middle Eastern indulgence. There are all manner of wraps and scrubs on offer (using organic local Shiffa products), while the Thai massage is, of course, particularly good. The Shiffa Cleansing Emerald Ritual is as indulgent a treatment as you'll find anywhere. **Map** 1 D3

Anantara Spa, Emirates Palace

Anantara Spa

02 690 9000

Emirates Palace, Al Ras Al Akhdar

spa.anantara.com

The Emirates Palace spa is just as elaborate and meticulously detailed as you would expect from its location. The soft earth tones and gorgeous Arabesque decor will immediately relax visitors, and the treatment rooms are large and airy. With steam rooms, Jacuzzis, an ice cave and a Moroccan hammam, the facilities are exactly as you'd expect from this opulent venue. Treatment highlights include a caviar facial, Elemis treatments and the royal hammam ritual. Couple's treatments are also available. **Map** 3 A2

Bodylines

02 656 4000

Yas Island Rotana, Yas Island West

rotana.com

You receive a warm welcome at the Bodylines fitness centre and, while the menu is limited to full body, hot stone or area specific massage, the facility is spa-like in appearance with its cool slate walls, aromatherapy scented air and serene, spacious layout. There is also a gym on-site that boasts a full compliment of workout equipment. **Map** 1 H3

CHI, The Spa

02 509 8900

Shangri-La Hotel, Qaryat Al Beri, Al Maqtaa

shangri-la.com

The spa within the Shangri-La has quickly established itself as one of the most beautiful in the city. Covered in black marble, the treatment and relaxation rooms are quietly comfortable and relaxing. A wide range of treatments are available, and CHI prides itself on its half-day 'journeys' that include several treatments as well as a meal. **Map** 2 D2

Eden Spa & Health Club

02 644 6666
Le Meridien Abu Dhabi,
Tourist Club Area
lemeridienabudhabi.com

The ultimate in stress relief and personal pampering, treatments include sessions in the aquamedic pool, various massages, aromatherapies, facials, mineral baths, seaweed wraps, and Turkish baths as well as its specialities of Lithos Therapy and Ayurveda. There is also a health club on-site, along with a tranquil beach and pools to relax in. **Map** 3 G3

ESPA At Yas Viceroy

02 697 4372
Yas Viceroy, Yas Island West
viceroyhotelsandresorts.com

The UK's ESPA is something of a byword for luxurious indulgence and ESPA at Yas Viceroy is the dictionary definition of a modern, urban spa. From welcome to goodbye, it's a classy and professional operation, and the treatments on offer are vast – signature treatments, facials, dedicated male treatments, a ladies' hammam, and more than 30 massages, wraps and scrubs; the range of combination journeys and 'escapes' offer good value. **Map** 1 H3

Hiltonia Health Club & Spa

02 681 1900
Hilton Abu Dhabi, Corniche
hilton.com

A haven of tranquillity. Apart from the usual aromatherapy and reflexology treatments, it also offers Indian head massage and a range of hydro bath treatments. Alternatively, you can choose from a menu of special packages, which combine body treatments and facials, and include the use of facilities (sauna, eucalyptus steam room and Jacuzzi). **Map** 3 A2

Iridium Spa

02 498 8888

St Regis Saadiyat Island Resort, Saadiyat Island

stregissaadiyatisland.com

Whites, beiges and browns, along with the natural stone and wood finishes, give Iridium a feeling of rustic pampering perfection. The treatment menu is fairly expansive (and expensive) but rather than provide a one-size-fits-all therapy, each massage, scrub and wrap is tailored to the client's wants and needs. **Map** 1 D1

Mizan

02 617 0000

Hilton Capital Grand Abu Dhabi, Al Madina Al Riyadiya

hilton.com

Mizan is a real surprise. The cavernous spa is one of Abu Dhabi's biggest and arguably its best equipped, with the usual wet zones, saunas and Jacuzzis appearing alongside experiential showers, lovely plunge pools, a Vichy shower suite and a deluxe hammam area. The decor throughout is soft, airy and spacious, creating a nice, relaxed mood that differs from the standard spa 'chill out'. **Map** 2 B2

Monte-Carlo Beach Club

02 656 3500

Saadiyat Beach, Saadiyat Island

montecarlobeachclub.ae

For the uninitiated, the best way to think of Monte-Carlo Beach Club, Saadiyat is as a boutique five-star hotel without the bedrooms. If you tire of the beautiful pool and the stretch of private beach, head for the spa – just as boutique, the lovely treatment rooms are ideal for relaxing massages or scrubs, while the adjoining changing rooms and wet areas

Clockwise from top: Bodylines Health & Fitness Centre, Eden Spa & Health Club, serene moments

SELECTION

(separate women's and men's) include a palatial Jacuzzi, sauna, steam room; there are inside and outside day beds for a bit of a snooze or a spot of reading, or you can head to the golden sands of the beach afterwards. **Map** 1 D1

Rayana Spa

02 596 1100

Hyatt Capital Gate Abu Dhabi, Al Safarat

hyatt.com

When you're located on the 19th floor of a record-breaking tower, it'd be a crime to hide the surroundings under the typical dark spa blinds and candlelight. The five treatment rooms at Rayana embrace the location, with some nice Arabian touches added too. Each treatment room has a full complement of facilities, including private changing and showers, and the atmosphere here is relaxing and adult. In line with the ADNEC location, there's a great range of male-specific and express treatments for busy executives.
Map 2 A2

The SPA, Radisson Blu

02 656 2494

Radisson Blu Hotel, Yas Island West

radissonblu.com

Many of Abu Dhabi's spas reach exceptional levels, so factors like organisation, comfort and customer service take on extra importance. The SPA has them all down to an art. Arrive early and enjoy the Jacuzzi, steam room or sauna then give your body over to the capable therapists. The aromatherapy massages and Anne Semonin facials are a cut above, but if you've a couple of hours to spare, try the signature Radisson Blu Formulation. The ladies' Jacuzzi has a very pleasant view across the mangroves towards the city. **Map** 1 H3

Talise Spa

02 811 5888
Jumeirah At Etihad Towers, Al Ras Al Akhdar jumeirah.com

Talise is cavernous but the decor maintains a feeling of intimacy, throughout relaxation areas, private treatment rooms and the Turkish hammam. Indulgent scrubs, wraps, baths and massages are available from excellent therapists. If you're able to splash out or preparing for a special occasion (hint hint, brides-to-be), try one of the signature rituals – they cost the earth but will make your year. **Map** 3 A2

Zayna Spa

02 495 3822
Grand Millennium Al Wahda, Al Dhafra millenniumhotels.com

An array of facial and body treatments for both men and women are on offer at the new Zayna Spa. The luxurious, Asian themed venue has no less than 10 treatment rooms, and the spacious lounge area is perfect for relaxing after the pampering is finished. The packages vary from 30 minute quick treats to five hours of indulgence. **Map** 3 E5

Zen The Spa At Rotana

02 697 9000
Beach Rotana Abu Dhabi, Tourist Club Area rotana.com

Spacious and comfortable, descending into Zen is like disappearing down a rabbit hole of relaxation. If it can be scrubbed, wrapped, treated or massaged, then it's on the menu; signature treatments, such as pregnancy, rejuvenation and immune boosting massages, are excellent value. Each room has character and the suites, with colossal changing rooms, showers and baths, are luxury defined. **Map** 3 G4

Shopping

Capital Expenditure	188
Where To Go For…	192
Souks & Markets	196
Shopping Malls	200

Capital Expenditure

From enormous malls selling modern marvels to traditional souks brimming with exotic treasures, Abu Dhabi's shopping scene is the epitome of variety.

Shopping plays a big role in everyday life in this part of the world and, during the hotter months, the malls are oases of cool in the sweltering summer weather. The combination of Abu Dhabi's historical position on many ancient trade routes, coupled with the mix of nationalities passing through the city today, make it a shopping destination of choice for bargain hunters, collectors, souvenir seekers and shopaholics alike. Not only will you find a huge selection of mainstream items, authentic antiques and some unusual discoveries, all at excellent prices, but with shops staying open late into the evenings you can really shop at leisure.

Carpets, gold, spices and wooden antiques are all hot Items that find their way into many a home-bound tourist's luggage. It's up to you whether you want to spend thousands on a genuine antique or finely woven silk carpet, or whether you want to use your pocket change to buy a few cheap souvenirs. Many stores can arrange to ship your purchases back to your home country.

The size and architecture of Abu Dhabi's malls can be a surprise to some visitors. These huge structures are spacious and fully air-conditioned, and packed with a range of international brands. Apart from everyday shops like supermarkets, clothing stores and electronics outlets, most malls also have several shops selling local souvenirs, carpets and perfumes. Malls are much more than just places to shop equipped; with a range of entertainment and leisure facilities they are meeting points for families and friends – which makes them perennially popular.

If you're after a more authentic Arabian shopping experience, head for the traditional markets, or souks (p.196). Apart from an eclectic range of goods for sale, the markets are great for photo opportunities and for the bustling atmosphere that you can see, hear and smell all at once. Items to look out for in the souks include spices, silks, perfumes, souvenirs and antiques. Often, shops specialising in certain products can be found side by side, so it's easy to compare prices. If you find a brand name item selling for an unbelievable price, it could well be a fake. Souks are usually open from 08:00 to 13:00 and 16:00 to 19:00, except Fridays when they only open in the afternoon.

Sizing

Figuring out your size is fairly straightforward. International sizes are often printed on garment labels or the store will usually have a conversion chart on display. Otherwise, a UK size is always two higher than a US size (so a UK 10 is a US 6). To convert European sizes into US sizes, subtract 32 (so a European 38 is actually a US 6). To convert European sizes into UK sizes, a 38 is roughly a 10. As for shoes, a woman's UK 6 is a European 39 or US 8.5 and a men's UK 10 is a European 44 or a US 10.5. If in doubt, ask for help.

Bargaining

Bargaining is still common practice in the souks; you'll need to give it a go to get the best prices. Before you take the plunge, try to get an idea of prices from a few shops, as there can often be significant differences. Once you've decided how much you are willing to spend, offer an initial bid that is roughly around half that price. Stay laidback and vaguely disinterested. When your initial offer is rejected (and it will be), keep going until you reach an agreement or until you have reached your limit. If the price isn't right, say so and walk out – the vendor will often follow and suggest a compromise. The more you buy, the better the discount. When the price is agreed, it is considered bad form to back out. While common in souks, bargaining isn't commonly accepted in malls and independent shops. However, use your discretion, as there may be some room to negotiate in places like jewellery stores and smaller electronics stores. Ask whether there is a discount on the marked price and you may end up with a bargain.

Shipping

Fortunately, many courier and shipping companies have spotted the opportunity to service those who have forgotten about airport baggage restrictions and offer good deals on shipping. You have the option of sending goods by airmail, courier or sea; for smaller items, or for those that have to be delivered quickly, air freight is better and the items can be tracked. Aramex (aramex.com), DHL (dhl.co.ae), Federal Express (fedex.com), TNT (tnt.com) and UPS (ups.com) are all present in Abu Dhabi.

Top: handicrafts and furniture on sale at the Iranian Souk; Bottom: a shop in the Carpet Souk

Where To Go For...

Art

Abu Dhabi is not well known historically for its galleries, but the capital's art scene is beginning to boom with branches of the Louvre and Guggenheim due to open in the next couple of years. Most of the galleries display an interesting mix of contemporary art by Arabic and international artists, and many of the works are for sale. The Folklore Gallery (folkloregallery.net) is a great place for browsing, with displays of local pottery and art, and for having framing done; there's a wide range of frames and the craftsmanship is high. Gallery One in Souk Qaryat Al Beri sells a selection of stylish photographs and canvas prints (g-1.com). If it's a keepsake you're after, then look out for Explorer's stunning Sheikh Zayed Grand Mosque posters.

Carpets

Abu Dhabi boasts a huge range of carpets, which are available in various colours, designs, materials and prices. Traditionally, carpets come from Iran, Pakistan, Turkey, China and Central Asia. While salesmen are generally helpful and honest, it helps if you know a little bit about carpets before you agree on a price. As a rough guide, the higher the number of knots per square inch, the higher the price and the better the quality. Hand-made carpets also fetch a higher price. Most vendors will happily unroll carpet after carpet, discussing its history and merits at length. Don't feel obliged to purchase just because he has broken a sweat, but if you do want to buy, stick to your budget and bargain as hard as you can.

Gold

The UAE is justifiably known as one of the best places in the world to buy gold, and the capital leads the way. Gold in Abu Dhabi is sold according to the fixed daily international gold rate, which is not up for negotiation. However, when buying a piece of jewellery a charge is added for craftsmanship and this is where your bargaining power increases. A popular souvenir is to have your name in Arabic made into a gold pendant; most jewellery shops offer this service in white or yellow gold.

There are jewellery shops in most malls, but if you want the best range and more room to bargain, head to either Hamdan Street near the Liwa Centre, or to the Madinat Zayed Shopping Centre & Gold Centre (p.207).

Souvenirs

You may find items for sale, such as ivory, which are subject to international trade and import bans or contravene the CITES convention. Don't risk taking them with you. If you wish to buy souvenirs that promote and preserve local handicrafts, and not break the law, see the companies listed at Made in the UAE (madeintheuae.com). Colourful pashminas are widely available and they are great as lightweight shawls (for when the weather is warm but the air conditioning is cold). While genuine pashminas are made from the wool of the pashmina goat (found only in Kashmir, India), most pashminas today are made of a cotton or silk mix, and the ratio dictates the price. Souvenir shops usually have several shelves stacked high with a kaleidoscope of colours. Compare prices in a few shops to get a feel for quality and range, and have a go at bargaining before you agree on a price.

Shisha pipes are widely available in souvenir shops and hypermarkets, and the tobacco comes in a variety of flavours. Wooden trinket boxes, photo frames and carvings are popular and can be found in souvenir shops. They are often decorated with brass or polished camel bone. The Hamdan Centre (p.206) has an excellent range of shoes and handbags at bargain prices, should you fancy a spree.

Tailoring

There are many tailors in Abu Dhabi and most operate from small shops tucked away down side streets. It is well worth buying a few metres of fabric and getting something made up to your measurements – tailors can copy a pattern, a garment, or even a photograph. Standards of workmanship vary, so ask around to get recommendations of good tailors.

Most tailors have a stack of fashion catalogues that you can look through to get some ideas, and once you've chosen something they will be able to tell you how much fabric you need to buy. They will probably provide the little extras like zips, buttons and cotton.

Confirm the price before the tailor starts working on the item. In most cases you'll find that the cost of having something made is very reasonable, although it obviously depends on the intricacy of the workmanship required. When the garment is finished, you will be able to try it on and have minor adjustments made if necessary.

Souks & Markets

These traditional markets have evolved from dusty hubs of trade into bustling tourist attractions packed with a fascinating collection of items.

Souk is the Arabic word for a market or a place where any kind of goods are bought or exchanged. Historically, dhows from the Far East, China, Ceylon and India would offload their cargo, and the goods would be haggled over in the souks adjacent to the docks. Souks were the social and commercial centres of life here, providing places to meet friends and socialise outside the family.

Over the years, the items on sale have diversified dramatically from spices, silks and perfumes, to include electronic goods and the latest kitsch consumer trends. Traditionally, the souks developed organically and were a maze of shady alleyways, with small shops opening on to the paths. Nowadays most of these have been redesigned and replaced by large, air-conditioned developments. Although Abu Dhabi's souks aren't as fascinating as others in the Arab world, such as Fes

Keep The Khanjar

If you buy a khanjar (traditional dagger), it will need to be packed in your luggage to go in the hold – even if it's been framed – and you may still need to declare it. If you try to carry it in your hand luggage it will be confiscated.

in Morocco or Mutrah in Oman, they are worth a visit for their bustling atmosphere, eclectic variety of goods, and the traditional way of doing business. Some of the souks have porters who will follow you around and carry your goods for a few dirhams (agree on a price though, before they start).

Al Ain Camel & Livestock Souk

Nr Bawadi Mall, Zayed Bin Sultan St, Al Ain

One of the only camel markets left in the UAE, this is a great way to experience a bit of local trading, while camel blankets make great souvenirs. The market now also contains the livestock market. **Map** 4 H9

Al Ain Souk

Zayed Bin Sultan St, Al Ain

Also known as the Central or Old Souk, the Al Ain Souk is a great place to explore, savour the local atmosphere, and practise your bargaining skills. The souk itself is a rather ramshackle affair but makes a refreshing change from many of the modern, rather sterile, air-conditioned markets that are appearing elsewhere across the UAE. **Map** 4 G8

Carpet Souk

Al Meena Rd, Al Meena

Yemeni mattresses and machine-made carpets dominate, but bargains can be found if you're prepared to haggle. Some of the vendors will make Arabic 'majlis' cushions to order for a very reasonable price. This is also known as the Afghan Souk and is located near the main port area. **Map** 3 H2

Fish, Fruit & Vegetable Souk

Nr Iranian Souk, Al Meena

The day's catch is loaded onto the quayside and sold wholesale for the first two hours of trading (04:30 to 06:30), with smaller quantities sold after that. Even if you're not buying, the fish market makes an interesting stop as the atmosphere is electric, while the Fruit & Vegetable Souk across the road offers a more relaxed experience. **Map** 3 H1

Iranian Souk

Nr Fish, Fruit & Vegetable Souk, Al Meena

It may not be air-conditioned, but this souk is worth a visit for the fresh batches of Iranian goods (such as terracotta urns, decorative metal, cane and glass items), which arrive regularly by dhow or barge. It is also known as Al Meena Souk. As it's part of a working port, photography is prohibited. **Map** 3 H1

Mwaifa Souk

Sheikh Khalifa Bin Zayed St, Al Ain

This modern market consists of a long strip of handy shops, with an intriguing mix of chain stores and independents, including a bakery, a baby shop and a toy shop. **Map** 4 F8

Souk Al Bawadi & Al Qaws

03 784 0000

Bawadi Mall, Al Ain

bawadimall.com

Connected to Bawadi Mall, Souk Al Bawadi has a heritage feel with stores selling traditional items and souvenirs. Souk Al Qaws has practical shops including banks and money exchanges. **Map** 4 H9

The Souk At Qaryat Al Beri

02 558 1670

Qaryat Al Beri, Al Maqtaa

soukqaryatalberi.com

This modern-day souk is a magnificent example of Arabian architecture and one of the first of its kind in the capital. The area holds a mix of local and international retail brands, coffee shops and a diverse range of restaurants. Abras wind through the canals providing transportation around the souk and the complex offers stunning alfresco dining options.
Map 2 D1

Souq Al Zaafarana

Nr Emirates International Hospital, Al Ain

A few years ago, Al Ain's traditional souk was handed a new home in the shape of Souk Al Zaafarana. This is now one of the largest and most popular souks in Al Ain. With more than 150 shops – the fruit and vegetable market alone has more than 90 shops – it offers a beguiling range of textiles, hand-crafted goods and perfumes. There is also a seafood restaurant and kids' play area. **Map** 4 F7

World Trade Center Central Market

02 810 7814

Nr Hamdan St, Markaziya East

wtcad.com

The Central Market Souk is part of the redevelopment that includes the new World Trade Center Mall. The architecture fuses traditional Arabic influences with modern design and the setting alone makes the centre worth the visit. In addition, The Souk is home to dozens of shops and boutiques, and there's also a good mix of restaurants and cafes.
Map 3 E2

Shopping Malls

The most popular malls are more than just places to shop; in the evenings, and especially at the weekends, they are places to meet, eat and parade.

Abu Dhabi Cooperative Society

02 667 9222

Al Khalidiya

adcoops.com

This shopping centre has been around for some time; its main draws are Splash (trendy, inexpensive fashions), Shoe Mart (huge range of shoes), Lifestyle (funky gifts and much more) and The Baby Shop. Other smaller shops include computer suppliers and ladies' fashion outlets. **Map** 3 C3

Abu Dhabi Mall

02 645 4858

Nr Beach Rotana Abu Dhabi, Tourist Club Area

abudhabi-mall.com

This is one of the main attractions of the Abu Dhabi shopping scene. With more than 220 retail outlets spread across four floors, it attracts over 25,000 visitors each day. It's range of international high-street stores and local brands should keep most shopaholics happy. Abu Dhabi Mall is not just a shopping destination – with restaurants on every floor, a six-screen Cineplex, a huge foodcourt and a children's play area, there's something to keep the whole family happy. It also hosts exciting promotional exhibitions throughout the year, including a popular Christmas Market. The mall has a sizeable carpark. **Map** 3 G3

Top: The Souk at Central Market; Bottom: Abu Dhabi Mall

Al Ain Mall

03 766 0333
Al Qwaitat St, Al Ain
alainmall.net

Al Ain Mall has changed the face of shopping in the 'garden city'. With over 100,000 square metres of retail and entertainment space spread across three floors, this bright, modern mall has stores selling a wide range of souvenirs, jewellery and every-day items. The family entertainment area has a 12 lane bowling alley as well as a multi-screen cinema; in addition, there is an ice-skating rink on the ground floor.
Map 4 H8

Al Raha Mall

02 556 2229
Off Abu Dhabi-Dubai Rd, Al Raha
al-rahamall.com

The nearest mall to Yas Island, although the large new Deerfields Townsquare recently opened just past Yas on the way to Dubai. It's good for visitors staying on the mainland and popular with locals. While not as oppulent as other malls, it offers excellent options for souvenirs and essentials like food, toys, and sports and electric goods. It's right next to Al Raha Hotel too so is super convenient for guests there.
Map 1 H4

Al Wahda Mall

02 443 7070
Nr Al Wahda Sports Club, Hazaa Bin Zayed The First St, Al Dhafra
alwahda-mall.com

With nearly hundreds of stores (a recent extension saw the mall double in size), a hypermarket and foodcourt, Al Wahda is an impressive addition to Abu Dhabi's retail landscape. The enormous mall features fashion, electronics, jewellery and health and beauty stores across two floors. There is parking for more than 1,700 cars. **Map** 3 E5

Bawabat Al Sharq Mall

02 445 2525

Nr Baniyas Police Station, Baniyas East — bawabatalsharq.ae

A shopper's paradise, consisting of more than 300 stores, a Carrefour hypermarket, a Grand Cinemas complex, and a Wanasa family entertainment centre. As well as fashion staples, such as H&M, Springfield and Centrepoint, there's a Victoria's Secret and the city's first branch of Gocco (02 586 8120) – the kids' fashion brand from Spain. In total, there are 22 food and drink outlets scattered throughout the foodcourt and the rest of the mall. **Map** 1 H7

Bawadi Mall

03 784 0000

Zayed Bin Sultan St, Al Ain — bawadimall.com

The Bawadi Mall has set high standards for the city's shopping scene. Browse through 400 shops, representing both international and regional brands and a range of high-street and designer names. For refreshment, head to the foodcourt or one of the many casual dining outlets throughout the mall. There is also entertainment for the family including a ski village, rollercoaster, an eight-screen cinema and a bowling alley. The Heritage Village features beautiful Islamic architecture and a range of shops selling souvenirs in a traditional market. The mall also has two outdoor markets, Souk Al Bawadi and Al Qaws (p.198). **Map** 4 H9

Boutik Mall, Sun & Sky Towers

02 674 7850

Shams Abu Dhabi, Al Reem Island facebook.com/boutikmall

A sort of mini-mall on Reem Island and home to the capital's first Waitrose supermarket. There are also food and drink outlets such as La Brioche Café, Yogen Früz and Macondo Colombian Café. For a high end shopping experience, the Galleria on neighbouring Maryah Island is an exclusive destination with top global designer brands and a selection of very good food outlets. **Map** 1 C2

Dalma Mall

02 550 6111

Nr Mohammed Bin Zayed City,
Abu Dhabi-Tarif-Al Ain Highway, Mussafah dalmamall.ae

Anchored by Carrefour, Home Centre, Matalan and one of the country's biggest Marks & Spencer stores, it is also home to the usual array of international brands, like H&M, American Eagle, Debenhams, Jumbo Electronics and Topshop. As for entertainment, there is an international foodcourt that has branches of Soy Express, Koala, Special Juice Bar and Yogen Früz, with seating for 500 visitors. In addition, mall-goers can enjoy a giant 14 screen CineStar Cineplex, while kids will love the Fun City play zone. **Map** 1 F7

Fotouh Al Khair Centre

02 681 1130

Shk Rashid Bin Saeed Al Maktoum St, Markaziya East

This is home to some favourite brands including Marks & Spencer. With a host of other outlets selling everything from watches to lingerie and children's fashions, this mall buzzes in the evenings and at the weekends. **Map** 3 E2

Hamdan Centre

02 632 8555

Shk Hamdan Bin Mohd St, Markaziya East

Something of an institution on Abu Dhabi's shopping scene and located in the heart of the city, this vibrant centre is a good place to buy clothing, leather, shoes, sports equipment and touristy knick-knacks, all at reasonable prices. Practise your bargaining skills here to get a good discount. **Map** 3 E2

Khalidiyah Mall

02 635 4000

King Khalid Bin Abdulaziz Saeed St, Al Khalidiyah

khalidiyahmall.com

The mall should not to be confused with the older, smaller Khalidiyah Centre just up the road. It is designed in a distinctive Islamic architectural style and is spread out over three floors. Home to over 160 stores, a large branch of Lulu Hypermarket can be found on the first and second floors. Other highlights include Debenhams and BHS, plentiful cafes and restaurants as well as a large foodcourt. The third floor offers a few entertainment options; Sparky's Family Fun Centre (02 635 4317) is an amusement centre which includes rides and a bowling alley, and the nine-screen CineRoyal cinema. **Map** 3 C3

Khalifa Centre

Nr Abu Dhabi Co-Operative Society, Tourist Club Area

This mall is teeming with regional craft and souvenir shops, as well as outlets selling Persian and Baluchi carpets. It's an essential stop if you're looking for souvenirs but would rather not visit the souks. **Map** 3 G3

Liwa Centre

02 632 0344

Shk Hamdan Bin Mohd St, Markaziya East

This is the location to head to on Hamdan Street for jewellery, clothes, makeup, perfume and more. It's a spot where men and women can get glammed up on the cheap while you'll also find souvenirs aplenty. Book lovers should head for House of Prose, an excellent second-hand bookshop. **Map** 3 E2

LuLu Center

02 678 0707

Shk Zayed Bin Sultan St, Nr Corniche Hospital, Markaziya East

luluhypermarket.com

This is an absolute Aladdin's cave, selling almost everything under the sun – from consumer electronics, sportswear and children's toys, to stationery, clothing, cosmetics and travel accessories. Some items are real bargains, an awful lot are pretty tatty, but it's fun to explore. **Map** 3 G2

Madinat Zayed Shopping Centre & Gold Centre

02 633 3311

Nr Post Office, East Rd, Madinat Zayed

madinatzayed-mall.com

Shopaholics will love this mall – it has more than 400 outlets selling just about everything an avid shopper could dream of. Next to the main mall, Homes r Us is popular for furniture and home accessories. Japanese store Daiso has an eclectic range of stock and most items are just Dhs.6. The Madinat Zayed Gold Centre, adjacent to the main mall, glitters with the finest gold, diamond and pearl jewellery. Plus, the supervised toddlers' area and the games arcade will keep the kids entertained while you shop. **Map** 3 E3

Marina Mall
02 681 2310
Kasser Al Amwaj, Corniche St, Breakwater
marinamall.ae

Situated on the Breakwater, Marina Mall is one of Abu Dhabi's biggest shopping centres and offers plenty of entertainment options. It houses a tower with a viewing platform and restaurant, a nine-screen CineStar complex, Fun City amusement centre for the kids and an ice rink. There are a host of high-street stores, as well as numerous luxury brands, such as Louis Vuitton and Fendi, plus restaurants and coffee shops. **Map** 3 B1

MultiBrand
02 621 9700
Nr Shk Hamdan Bin Mohd St & Baniyas St, Markaziya East

This large, open-plan location is home to a good number of well-known international shops. In fact, its store list sounds like it has come straight from a British high street, with shops such as Mothercare, Claire's, Next and Oasis. For footwear there's the stylish Milano. **Map** 3 F3

Rotana Mall
02 681 4433
Al Khaleej Al Arabi St, Al Khalidiyah

Near the Corniche, this dinky mall is best known for a few shops selling antiques, carpets, handicrafts, Arabic pottery and wall hangings. There are some nice pieces here. **Map** 3 C3

Marina Mall

Department Stores

Marks & Spencer

02 621 3646

Fotouh Al Khair Centre,
Markaziya East

marksandspencerme.com

One of the best known brands from the UK, M&S, as it is known, sells men's, women's and children's clothes and shoes, along with a small, but ever popular, selection of food. The store is famous for its selection of underwear and has a reputation for quality. It's also a great place to stock up on basics. Branches in the UAE carry selected ranges which include the Per Una range – high-street chic – as well as more classic lines. Also has branches in Marina Mall and Dalma Mall. **Map** 3 E2

Next

02 645 4832

Abu Dhabi Mall, Tourist Club Area

next.co.uk

Next is a popular British chain that now has a number of stores in the UAE. Each branch stocks a range of quality high-street fashion for men, women and children, as well as shoes, underwear and accessories. It's a great place to go clothes shopping for all occasions, whether you need casual daywear, office attire, party outfits or even semi-formal evening wear. The kids' clothing section is excellent catering for newborns to teenagers and has a good range of children's shoes. **Map** 3 G3

Studio R

02 681 7676

Marina Mall, Breakwater

rshlimited.com

Studio R sells a selection of brands catering to those with an active lifestyle. With a range of well-known clothing labels (Mango, Bebe, Massimo Dutti, Nautica, Tag Heuer, Lacoste and Rockport), and sports brands (adidas, Puma and Reebok), Studio R has created its own niche in Abu Dhabi. Look out for sales throughout the year, when prices are heavily discounted. **Map** 3 B1

Woolworths

02 681 0881

Marina Mall, Breakwater

woolworths.co.za

This is a home away from home for South Africans – Woolworths in South Africa is similar to Marks & Spencer in the UK. It is renowned as the place to go for high-quality clothes, shoes and home textiles (towels and bedding). They also do a great range of accessories and underwear. In the

UAE, Woolworths may be slightly less impressive than the original stores, but the items are still high quality and the range offers something a little different to standard (UK) goods. **Map** 3 B1

Supermarkets & Hypermarkets

Abu Dhabi has a good range of stores and supermarkets stocking a wide selection of international and local produce. Prices vary dramatically; produce is imported from all over the world and some items cost twice as much as they would in their country of origin. There are plenty of 'corner shops' in residential areas, good for last-minute essentials. Popular food shops include the Abu Dhabi Co-operative Society (adcoops.com), which has branches all over the city. Abela is a superstore with a range of shops offering groceries, stationery, video rental, books and magazines, as well as dry-cleaning services. Spinneys (spinneys.co.ae) keeps the Brits happy with its Waitrose range, as well as other British

Big Spenders

The choice of local treasures and shopping pleasures means you may find your purchases exceed your luggage allowance. Many courier and shipping companies offer visitors good deals on shipping booty back home though. You can send by airmail, courier or sea; options include: Aramex (02 555 1911, aramex.com), DHL (800 4004, dhl.co.ae), Federal Express (800 33339, fedex.com/ae) and Empost (600 565 555, empostuae.com).

products, but the store also stocks a great range of South African, Australian and American products. Waitrose itself has opened a few of its own stores, mainly in the newer residential areas like Al Zeina at Al Raha Beach and on Reem Island. Carrefour (carrefouruae.com) is a huge hypermarket and part of a large French chain with a number of locations around the city. It sells everything from cheap shoes to toothpaste, as well as a good selection of fruit, vegetables, fish and seafood, and is a good place to look for hard-to-find western brands or specialist foods.

Independent & Noteworthy Stores

Abu Dhabi's independent shopping scene isn't hugely varied, but there are a few hidden gems and fascinating stores selling regional specialities and clothing items you won't have seen everywhere. The Souk At Qaryat Al Beri (p.199) has a few independent outlets which are worth exploring, or you could try your luck at Central Market (p.199). La Casa Del Habano (02 644 1505) in Abu Dhabi Mall is worth a visit if you are after a hit of tobacco. Also in the same mall is Marina Exotic Home Interiors (02 645 5488), a home furnishings specialist with pieces that reflect the region.

The canvas prints and beautifully framed photographs at Gallery One (g-1.com) make great souvenirs. Grafika (grafikaboutique.com) stocks non-mainstream, Arabian-inspired fashion items. Ounass (02 681 8667) is another store that appeals to the sophisticated party people of the UAE; it stocks lines from high-end designers such as Marchesa and Alberta Ferretti. The store has a branch in Marina Mall.

Shopping for exotic souvenirs

Going Out

After Hours	216
Entertainment	222
Venue Directory	226
Area Directory	230
Restaurants & Cafes	238
Bars, Pubs & Clubs	278

After Hours

Visitors should be pleasantly surprised with the nightlife in the emirate, whether you want to soak up the atmosphere or enjoy the party.

Cosmopolitan and bustling, Abu Dhabi has an excellent and ever-increasing variety of restaurants. From Moroccan to Mexican, Indian to Italian and everything in between, there really is something to suit every palate and budget.

Many of Abu Dhabi's best and most popular restaurants are located in hotels. These are pretty much the only outlets that can serve alcohol with your meal, although some clubs and associations are also permitted to do so. The taxes levied on alcohol translate into fairly high prices for drinks at a restaurant. You will rarely find a bottle of house wine for less than around Dhs.90, and a beer will probably cost you at least Dhs.25 but often more.

The Yellow Star

The little yellow star highlights venues that merit extra praise. It could be the atmosphere, the food, the cocktails, the music or the crowd, but whatever the reason, any review that you see with the star attached is somewhere considered a bit special.

However, there are quite a number of unlicensed independent restaurants throughout town that are excellent and shouldn't be ignored. 'Tourist' restaurants, mainly those located in hotels, are permitted to charge service fees. Tax and service charges can add an extra 16% to the bill so, to avoid a nasty surprise, check the small print on the menu to see whether these charges are included in the prices. If you want to reward the waiting staff directly then the standard rule of a 10% tip will be appreciated.

The capital may not have the quantity of outlets of a big city like New York, but there's plenty of variety to keep even the most ardent socialite happy. People tend to go out late in Abu Dhabi and usually not before 21:00. Even on week nights, kick-off is surprisingly late. If you're venturing out to Arabic nightclubs or restaurants before 23:00, you're likely to find them almost deserted, but bars like Pearls & Caviar (p.267) are boosting business.

Generally, cafes and restaurants close between 23:00 and 01:00, and most bars and nightclubs split between those that close 'early' at 01:00 and those who stay open 'late' until 02:00 or 03:00. Few are open all night.

Brunch & Other Deals

An integral part of life in the capital, the famous Friday brunch is a perfect event for a lazy start to the weekend. This is especially true once the hot weather arrives. Popular with all sections of the community, it provides Thursday night's revellers with a gentle awakening and some much needed nourishment. For families, brunch is a pleasant way to spend the earlier part of the day, especially since many venues organise a variety of fun activities for kids, allowing parents to fill themselves with fine food and drink, and to simply relax with friends. Prices are higher for the alcoholic drinks option.

Thursday and Friday nights are obviously busy, but you will also find that during the week many bars and restaurants offer promotions and special nights to attract customers, thus creating a lively atmosphere. Particularly popular is ladies' night, which is the busiest night of the week for some places (usually Tuesday night, but it varies from place to place). Women are given drink tokens at the door and the number varies from one to an endless supply, though it may be limited to certain types of drinks. This ploy certainly seems to attract male customers too.

Door Policy

There are a few considerations to heed when going out in Abu Dhabi: anyone who is rowdy may find their entry is refused (and drunken behaviour in public places can land you behind bars); large groups, single men and certain nationalities may have difficulty gaining admission, but breaking the group up or going in a mixed gender group can help. The minimum drinking age is 21.

Vegetarian

Vegetarians should be pleasantly surprised by the range and variety of veggie food that can be found in restaurants in Abu Dhabi. Although the main course of Arabic cuisine is dominated by meat, the staggering range of mezze (which are often vegetarian) and the general affection for fresh vegetables should offer enough variety to satisfy even the most ravenous herbivore.

Most outlets offer at least one or two veggie dishes. However, if you want a little more variety, choices include the numerous

Indian vegetarian restaurants catering to the large number of Indians who are vegetarian by religion (see Indian on p.227). These offer diverse styles of cooking and a range of tasty dishes – for vegetarians, this option is hard to beat. Other highlights include loads of excellent Italian (p.227), Mexican (p.228) and international restaurants (p.227) all over the city. Some of Abu Dhabi's cafes serve good vegetarian food, especially THE One (p.265).

A word of warning: if you are a strict veggie, confirm that your meal is completely meat free. Some restaurants cook their vegetarian selection with animal fat or on the same grill as the meat dishes.

Nightclubs

Abu Dhabi's nightclubs are busy from about 23:00 till the wee hours. The city has a reasonable number of dedicated nightclubs as well as numerous other venues that have several functions (bars or restaurants that, come late evening, turn into a packed joint where you can cut loose on the dancefloor). If you want to indulge in some real clubbing, head to the new O1NE Yas Island club or the neighbouring emirate of Dubai, which often hosts top international DJs.

Additionally, since you're in the Middle East, do not overlook the option of Arabic nightclubs. This is your chance to sample Arabic cuisine and enjoy a night of traditional entertainment, usually with a belly dancer, a live band and a singer. These venues start buzzing very late in the evening – a classic reflection of the Arabic way of starting late and finishing, well… later.

Street Food

Throughout the city, you will find roadside stands selling 'shawarma' (made from rolled pita bread filled with lamb or chicken that is carved from a rotating spit) and salad. Costing about Dhs.3 each, this is not only an inexpensive option but also well worth trying as an excellent alternative to the usual hamburger. Shawarma stands usually sell other dishes too, such as 'foul' (a paste made from fava beans) and 'falafel' (small savoury balls of deep fried chickpeas). While most shawarma stands offer virtually the same thing, slight differences make some stand out from the rest. People are often adamant that their particular favourite serves, for example, the best falafel in town. Every restaurant has its own way of doing things and you might find that the smallest, most low key restaurants can be excellent value.

Arabian Experience

There are ample opportunities to enjoy traditional Arabic cuisine. Most of Abu Dhabi's cuisine hails from Lebanon and Syria. Tabouleh (chopped parsley with bulgur, tomato and herbs), fattoush (tangy salad seasoned with sumac and topped with toasted pita), arayes (grilled flat bread with spiced meat in the middle) and many kinds of grilled, skewered meat can be found in any Arabic restaurant and are great introductions to local cuisine (p.12). The full Arabian experience can be enjoyed in the desert, on a safari, where you will be entertained by a belly dancer, smoke shisha and dine on a full array of Arabic delights under the stars. Most tour operators (p.152) offer a desert dinner experience.

Entertainment

The variety of entertainment in Abu Dhabi is growing with an annual film festival and international music acts now major parts of the events calendar.

Cinema

A trip to the cinema is one of the most popular forms of entertainment in the Emirates and movie buffs are relatively well catered for, although showings are generally limited to the latest Arabic, Asian or Hollywood films. Most of the bigger cinemas, VOX Cinemas (voxcinemas.com) and Grand Cinemas (grandcinemas.com), are multi-screen mega sites, while the older cinemas tend to have fewer screens. Both companies have several branches in Al Ain and Abu Dhabi. For movie times, check the daily newspapers as well as Entertainment Plus, the weekly magazine that is published with Gulf News every Wednesday. A handy website for checking movies and show times is movies.theemiratesnetwork.com. Movie release dates vary considerably with new Hollywood films reaching the UAE anywhere between four weeks to six months after release in the United States.

Inside, the air conditioners are usually on high and it can become very cold, so make sure you take something warm to wear. At weekends, there are extra shows at midnight or 01:00 – check the press for details. Tickets can be reserved, but usually have to be collected an hour before the show and sales are cash only. However, with so many screens around now, you will often find cinemas half empty, except for the first couple of days after the release of an eagerly awaited blockbuster.

Abu Dhabi Film Festival (p.57) is a big highlight on the cultural calendar and cinema screenings and events include a great selection of international films. In 2014, the film festival will take place from 16 to 25 October.

Comedy

The comedy scene in Abu Dhabi is, unfortunately, quite limited. However, there are regular visits from Dubai-based company The Laughter Factory (thelaughterfactory.com), as well as the occasional comical theatre production or one-off event. Comedy shows tend to be aimed at the British population, so other nationalities may not always get the joke. Events are often promoted only a short time before they actually take place, so keep your ears to the ground for what's coming up.

Live Music

Recent years have seen a significant upturn in the music scene. Emirates Palace (p.68) hosted a number of international artists including Shakira, George Michael, Alicia Keyes, Bon Jovi, Justin Timberlake, Christina Aguilera and Coldplay. The national exhibition centre ADNEC (adnec.ae) has also put on numerous big concerts and dance events.

The du Arena on Yas Island has more recently become the venue of choice, capable of holding thousands of music lovers in a well organised open air venue. It regularly hosts big-name gigs such as the Rolling Stones, Rihanna and Jay Z, as well as the huge concerts organised during the

Formula 1 race weekend. Club events, such as Ministry of Sound nights, have also taken place in Abu Dhabi, and the Abu Dhabi Music & Arts Foundation (admaf.org) has hosted several cultural events. The Abu Dhabi Classics programme which runs throughout the winter months is well attended (abudhabiclassics.com) too. Moreover, occasional events like the Jazz Festival Festival in Dubai (organised by Chillout Productions, chilloutproductions.com) are not to be missed. If you don't mind travelling to Dubai the beachfront Sandance gigs on Palm Jumeirah are a fantastic way to watch top international bands like The Killers and Jamiroquai. At different times of the year (mainly in winter), major sporting events, concerts and festivals feature international artists, bands and classical musicians and Abu Dhabi's Corniche has hosted a number of free gigs.

Promoters rarely have long-term programmes and details are only available about a month in advance. For details of events, check the daily press or monthly magazines, or askexplorer.com.

Theatre

The theatre scene in Abu Dhabi is rather quiet, with fans relying chiefly on touring companies and the occasional amateur dramatics performance. The amateur theatre, namely the Abu Dhabi Dramatic Society (abudhabidrama.com), always welcomes new members either on stage or behind the scenes. There is also the occasional murder mystery dinner where you are encouraged to display your Thespian skills by being part of the performance.

Jazz Festival

Venue Directory

Cafes & Restaurants

American	49er's The Gold Rush	p.239
	Heroes	p.255
American Bars	Rock Bottom Cafe	p.270
Asian	Cho Gao	p.250
	Quest	p.268
Asian Subcontinent	Jing Asia	p.256
Belgian	Belgian Beer Cafe	p.246
Brazilian	Chamas Churrascaria & Bar	p.249
Buffet	Arabesque	p.244
Cafes & Coffee Shops	Gerard Patisserie	p.254
	Havana Cafe	p.254
	Le Boulanger	p.260
	Nolu's Cafe	p.265
	Palm Lounge	p.266
	Riviera	p.270
	THE One	p.265
	Zyara Cafe	p.277
Chinese	Bam Bu!	p.245
	Shang Palace	p.271
Contemporary Asian	Noodle Box	p.265
Dinner Cruises	Al Dhafra	p.241
Emirati	Al Arish	p.240
	Al Datrah Restaurant	p.241
European	Assymetri	p.244
	Diablito	p.250
	Ornina	p.265
Far Eastern	Hakkasan	p.254
	The Wok	p.276
French	Bord Eau	p.249

	Le Beaujolais	p.258
	Le Bistrot	p.259
Fusion	Teatro	p.274
Indian	Angar	p.244
	India Palace	p.256
	Kwality	p.258
	Nihal Restaurant	p.264
	Rangoli	p.270
	Tanjore	p.272
	Ushna	p.275
International	Al Fanar	p.242
	Assymetri	p.244
	Sevilla	p.271
	Sofra Bld	p.272
	The Garden Restaurant	p.252
	The Village Club	p.275
	Zest	p.276
Italian	Amalfi	p.242
	Biancorosso Pizza	p.248
	Casa Romana Restaurant	p.249
	Filini	p.251
	Frankie's Italian Restaurant & Bar	p.252
	Il Porto	p.255
	La Mamma	p.258
	Mezzaluna	p.262
	Pappagallo	p.267
	Porto Bello	p.268
	Prego's	p.268

	Spaccanapoli Ristorante	p.272
Japanese	Benihana	p.248
	Kazu	p.256
	Wasabi	p.276
Lebanese	Li Beirut	p.260
Mediterranean	18°	p.238
	Beach House	p.246
	Pearls & Caviar	p.267
Mexican	Amerigos	p.243
	El Sombrero	p.250
Middle Eastern	Al Birkeh	p.240
	Atayeb	p.245
	Barouk	p.245
	Lebanese Flower	p.260
	Mawal	p.261
	Min Zaman	p.262
Moroccan	Agadir	p.239
Polynesian	Trader Vic's	p.274
	Trader Vic's	p.274
Portuguese	Vasco's	p.275
Seafood	Aquarium	p.244
	Finz	p.251
	Fishmarket	p.252
Steakhouses	18Oz	p.238
	55&5th, The Grill	p.239
	Blue Grill	p.248
	Marco Pierre White Steakhouse & Grill	p.261

	Rodeo Grill	p.271
	The Meat Co	p.262
	The Park Bar & Grill	p.267
Tex Mex	Paco's	p.282
Thai	Pachaylen	p.266
Vietnamese	Hoi An	p.255

Bars, Pubs & Clubs

Bars	Captain's Arms	p.278
	Havana Club	p.279
	Lemon & Lime	p.280
	Relax@12	p.282
	Stills Bar & Brasserie	p.284
	Y Bar	p.284
Cigar Bars	Cloud Nine - Cigar & Champagne Bar	p.278
	Cristal	p.279
Jazz Bars	SAX	p.283
	The Jazz Bar & Dining	p.280
Nightclubs	O1NE Yas Island	p.279
Pubs	Cooper's Bar & Restaurant	p.279
	PJ O'Reilly's	p.282
Sports Bars	Hickory's Sports Bar	p.280

Area Directory

Al Ain

Restaurants & Cafes

Arabesque	Danat Al Ain Resort	p.244
Casa Romana Restaurant	Hilton Al Ain	p.249
Min Zaman	Al Ain Rotana	p.262
Paco's	Hilton Al Ain	p.282
Tanjore	Danat Al Ain Resort	p.272
The Wok	Danat Al Ain Resort	p.276
Trader Vic's	Al Ain Rotana	p.274
Zest	Al Ain Rotana	p.276

Al Bateen

Restaurants & Cafes

Belgian Beer Cafe	InterContinental Abu Dhabi	p.246
Chamas Churrascaria & Bar	InterContinental Abu Dhabi	p.249
Fishmarket	InterContinental Abu Dhabi	p.252

Al Dhafra

Restaurants & Cafes

18Oz	One To One Hotel – The Village	p.238
Biancorosso Pizza	Y Tower, Nr Al Mamoura Bldg	p.248
Porto Bello	Grand Millennium Al Wahda	p.268
The Village Club	One To One Hotel – The Village	p.275

Al Khalidiyah

Restaurants & Cafes

Lebanese Flower	Nr Shk Zayed The First & Al Nahyan Sts	p.260

THE One	Khalidiya Theatre & Restaurant, Shk Zayed The First St	p.265
Zyara Cafe	Nr Hilton Corniche Residence, East Corniche St	p.277

Al Khubeirah

Restaurants & Cafes

Mawal	Hilton Abu Dhabi	p.261
Vasco's	Hilton Abu Dhabi	p.275

Bars, Pubs & Clubs

The Jazz Bar & Dining	Hilton Abu Dhabi	p.280

Al Maqtaa

Restaurants & Cafes

Bord Eau	Shangri-La Hotel, Qaryat Al Beri	p.249
Frankie's Italian Restaurant & Bar	Fairmont Bab Al Bahr	p.252
Hoi An	Shangri-La Hotel, Qaryat Al Beri	p.255
Marco Pierre White Steakhouse & Grill	Fairmont Bab Al Bahr	p.261
Pearls & Caviar	Shangri-La Hotel, Qaryat Al Beri	p.267
Shang Palace	Shangri-La Hotel, Qaryat Al Beri	p.271
Sofra Bld	Shangri-La Hotel, Qaryat Al Beri	p.272

The Meat Co	The Souk At Qaryat Al Beri	p.262
Ushna	The Souk At Qaryat Al Beri	p.275

Al Matar

Restaurants & Cafes

Pachaylen	Eastern Mangroves Hotel & Spa By Anantara	p.266
Teatro	Park Rotana Abu Dhabi	p.274

Bars, Pubs & Clubs

Cooper's Bar & Restaurant	Park Rotana Abu Dhabi	p.279

Al Meena

Restaurants & Cafes

Al Arish	Nr Mina Fish Market	p.240
Al Dhafra	Nr Meena Fish Market	p.241
Wasabi	Al Diar Mina Hotel	p.276

Al Raha

Restaurants & Cafes

Nolu's Cafe	Al Bandar Marina, Raha Beach	p.264
Ornina	Al Bandar Marina, Raha Beach	p.265
Sevilla	Al Raha Beach Hotel	p.271

Al Ras Al Akhdar

Restaurants & Cafes

Hakkasan	Emirates Palace	p.254
Li Beirut	Jumeirah At Etihad Towers	p.260

Mezzaluna	Emirates Palace	p.262
Quest	Jumeirah At Etihad Towers	p.268

Bars, Pubs & Clubs

Havana Club	Emirates Palace	p.280

Al Safarat

Restaurants & Cafes

18°	Hyatt Capital Gate Abu Dhabi	p.238

Bars, Pubs & Clubs

Relax@12	Aloft Abu Dhabi	p.282

Breakwater

Restaurants & Cafes

Al Datrah Restaurant	Heritage Village	p.241
Gerard Patisserie	Marina Mall	p.254
Havana Cafe	Nr Marina Mall, Hamdan St	p.254
Il Porto	Mirage Marine Complex, Nr Marina Mall	p.255

Madinat Zayed

Restaurants & Cafes

Nihal Restaurant	Nr Sands Hotel, Shk Zayed The Second St	p.264

Markaziya East

Restaurants & Cafes

Al Fanar	Le Royal Meridien Abu Dhabi	p.242
Amalfi	Le Royal Meridien Abu Dhabi	p.242
Cho Gao	Crowne Plaza Abu Dhabi	p.250
El Sombrero	Sheraton Abu Dhabi Hotel & Resort	p.250
Heroes	Crowne Plaza Abu Dhabi	p.255
Kwality	Nr National Bank of Fujairah	p.258
La Mamma	Sheraton Abu Dhabi Hotel & Resort	p.258
Le Beaujolais	Mercure Abu Dhabi Centre Hotel	p.258
Le Boulanger	Shk Hamdan Bin Mohd St	p.260
Palm Lounge	Le Royal Meridien Abu Dhabi	p.266
Spaccanapoli Ristorante	Crowne Plaza Abu Dhabi	p.272
The Garden Restaurant	Crowne Plaza Abu Dhabi	p.252

Bars, Pubs & Clubs

Cloud Nine – Cigar & Champagne Bar	Sheraton Abu Dhabi Hotel & Resort	p.278
Cristal	Millennium Hotel Abu Dhabi	p.279
PJ O'Reilly's	Le Royal Meridien Abu Dhabi	p.282
SAX	Le Royal Meridien Abu Dhabi	p.283

Saadiyat Island

Restaurants & Cafes

55&5th, The Grill	The St Regis Saadiyat Island Resort	p.239

Beach House	Park Hyatt Abu Dhabi Hotel & Villas	p.246
The Park Bar & Grill	Park Hyatt Abu Dhabi Hotel & Villas	p.267

Sas Al Nakhl Island

Restaurants & Cafes

Agadir	The Westin Abu Dhabi Golf Resort & Spa	p.239

Bars, Pubs & Clubs

Lemon & Lime	The Westin Abu Dhabi Golf Resort & Spa	p.281

Tourist Club Area

Restaurants & Cafes

49er's The Gold Rush	Al Diar Dana Hotel	p.239
Al Birkeh	Le Meridien Abu Dhabi	p.240
Bam Bu!	Abu Dhabi Marina & Yacht Club	p.245
Benihana	Beach Rotana Abu Dhabi	p.248
Finz	Beach Rotana Abu Dhabi	p.251
India Palace	Nr ADNOC, Al Salam St	p.256
Le Bistrot	Le Meridien Abu Dhabi	p.259
Pappagallo	Le Meridien Abu Dhabi	p.267
Prego's	Beach Rotana Abu Dhabi	p.268
Riviera	Nr Abu Dhabi Post Office	p.270
Rock Bottom Cafe	Al Diar Capital Hotel	p.270

★ Rodeo Grill	Beach Rotana Abu Dhabi	p.271
Trader Vic's	Beach Rotana Abu Dhabi	p.274

Bars, Pubs & Clubs

★ Captain's Arms	Le Meridien Abu Dhabi	p.278

Yas Island West
Restaurants & Cafes

Amerigos	Park Inn By Radisson Abu Dhabi, Yas Island Hotel	p.243
Angar	Yas Viceroy Abu Dhabi	p.244
Aquarium	Yas Marina	p.244
Assymetri	Radisson Blu Hotel, Abu Dhabi Yas Island	p.244
★ Atayeb	Yas Viceroy Abu Dhabi	p.245
Barouk	Crowne Plaza Abu Dhabi Yas Island	p.245
Blue Grill	Yas Island Rotana	p.248
Diablito	Yas Marina	p.250
Filini	Radisson Blu Hotel, Abu Dhabi Yas Island	p.251
Jing Asia	Crowne Plaza Abu Dhabi Yas Island	p.256
★ Kazu	Yas Viceroy Abu Dhabi	p.256
Noodle Box	Yas Viceroy Abu Dhabi	p.265
Rangoli	Yas Island Rotana	p.270

Bars, Pubs & Clubs

Hickory's Sports Bar	Yas Links Abu Dhabi	p.280
O1NE Yas Island	Yas Island	p.281
Stills Bar & Brasserie	Crowne Plaza Abu Dhabi Yas Island	p.284
Y Bar	Yas Island Rotana	p.284

Restaurants & Cafes

From top-notch fine dining and swanky bars to independent eateries and fastfood joints, there is a vast selection of eating options on offer in the emirate.

18°
Mediterranean

Hyatt Capital Gate Abu Dhabi, Al Safarat
02 596 1440

Located right on the most leaning section of the world's most leaning tower (hence the name), 18° is an evening venue worthy of visiting for more than just the awe-inspiring floor to ceiling views. Focused on Eastern Mediterranean cuisine, you can opt for Italian, Greek, Turkish, Syrian or Lebanese dishes, with the best flavours and produce hand-picked from those countries. Try the melt-in-the-mouth soft and sweet burrata cheese, crispy calamari or pickled halwayo to start; while the Syrian beef tenderloin is hard to beat for meat-lovers. **Map** 2 A2

18Oz
American Bistro

One To One Hotel – The Village, Al Dhafra
02 495 2000

18Oz specialises in mouth-watering steaks and chops, serving choice cuts of Angus beef drenched in a selection of eight sauces. Seafood appetisers and lamb, chicken and vegetarian main dishes can also be found on the menu. The modern decor and attentive service feels just right, and even the desserts are delicious. **Map** 3 F6

49er's The Gold Rush

American

Al Diar Dana Hotel, Tourist Club Area 02 645 6000

Centrally situated, this popular venue is often packed so get there early to enjoy an entire evening of entertainment. The rich timber finishes reflect a traditional ranch-style atmosphere and the food is delicious, with steaks that melt in the mouth. The service cannot be faulted and, with live music and reasonable prices, you can't go too wrong. **Map** 3 G2

55&5th, The Grill

Steakhouses

St Regis Saadiyat Island Resort, Saadiyat Island 02 498 8888

A high-end steakhouse that has been pulled straight from NYC. From the brick and leather decor, which makes it look like a modern gents' club, to the predominantly surf and turf inspired menu, this is upper-crust Big Apple through and through. Starters of foie gras, scallops or beef crudo are delicate but flavourful. Main courses are dominated by the excellent 'vintage beef from the aging room', although Scottish salmon, veal and lobster casserole also feature. There's an exceptional private chef's table perched in a 'wine library' high above the rest of the restaurant. **Map** 1 D1

Agadir

Moroccan

Westin Abu Dhabi Golf Resort & Spa, Khalifa City 02 616 9999

A delightfully atmospheric destination, this Moroccan restaurant combines both the ambience and cuisines of the Mediterranean and the Middle East to produce a rich and interesting menu. The starters are generally mezze in style, while there's a huge variety of main courses to choose from, although the tagines really take some beating. If anything can beat them, however, it'd be the shared lamb dishes – the mechoui and K'Taf M'Bakher are specialities of the house with the taste to prove it. **Map** 1 F4

Al Asalah Restaurant
Emirati

Heritage Village, Breakwater
02 681 2188

This traditional restaurant is a must. Where else can you stand under a windtower to test the earliest form of air conditioning while you sip on fresh fruit cocktails? You can also marvel at the contrast between the authentic artefacts of a bygone age and the glistening, ultra-modern cityscape across the turquoise waters on the Corniche. The menu features typical Arabic fare, and is served in a buffet format with hot and cold options including fresh fish, which is one of the best reasons to go there. **Map** 3 C1

Al Arish
Emirati

Nr Mina Fish Market, Al Meena
02 673 2266

For an authentic Arabian experience, look no further than this independent gem. At Al Arish, guests are instantly welcomed warmly and assisted in choosing from the attractive buffet selection of seafood, chicken and meat. The food at this restaurant is extremely fresh and also plentiful. A healthy choice of 'local' and traditional starters, mains and desserts can be washed down with freshly made fruit cocktails that are highly recommended. This is definitely a hidden gem. **Map** 3 H2

180z

Al Birkeh

Middle Eastern

Le Meridien, Tourist Club Area

02 644 6666

Widely touted as one of the best Arabic restaurants in town, it serves traditional Middle Eastern, complete with live music and a belly dancer. Start your culinary journey with hot and cold mezze before moving on to your main course of grilled meat or fish (and lots of it!). For the gastronomically brave only, the menu includes some exotic dishes such as raw liver, washed down with the strong aniseed drink 'arak'. **Map** 3 G3

Al Dhafra

Dinner Cruises

Nr Mina Fish Market, Al Meena

02 673 2268

This traditional dhow offers daily dinner cruises along the picturesque Corniche. The upper deck boasts a majlis and the lower air-conditioned deck can seat approximately 50 people.

A sumptuous menu includes lavish Arabic fare, and as you dine, the ethnic charm of the dhow and the serenity of the placid Arabian waters will ensure an unforgettable evening. **Map** 3 G1

Al Fanar

International

Le Royal Meridien Abu Dhabi, Markaziya East 02 674 2020

Professional, polite waiters who cater to your every whim enhance the feeling of other-worldliness at this revolving rooftop restaurant. The magnificent panoramic views are almost eclipsed by the extravagantly elaborate feast that is set before you. The hushed atmosphere and plush furnishings provide the perfect opportunity for gazing at stars or into a loved one's eyes. Al Fanar offers a truly impressive feast and a chance to see the city lights and Corniche from a unique angle. **Map** 3 F2

Amalfi

Italian

Le Royal Meridien, Markaziya East 02 674 2020

For a taste of authentic Italy, Amalfi offers fresh pasta, risotto and seafood cooked to perfection by a Sicilian chef. The chic, Italian-inspired design is open and airy, with big windows overlooking the terrace and pool. Traditional Italian music from the Sonata Duonello provides an excellent background to this stunning restaurant. The feel is unfussy, uncomplicated and simply elegant, lending itself to intimacy and romance. **Map** 3 F2

Amerigos

Mexican

Park Inn by Radisson Abu Dhabi, Yas Island West 02 656 2222

Suitable for casual or formal occasions, this spacious restaurant has a colourful, modern decor with a large TV at one end, dedicated mainly to sport. If you prefer, you can enjoy the view from the poolside dining area, which is also a little less smoky. Choose from traditional fajitas and quesadillas with fresh guacamole, or try meat and fish dishes, all served by friendly staff. Alternatively, just sip a long cocktail at the bar. A bustling restaurant that almost always results in a lively, sociable evening. **Map** 1 H3

Angar

Indian

Yas Viceroy, Yas Island West — 02 656 0600

The smell of divine spices will lead you straight to Angar. Authentic tastes of India mix with contemporary luxury, served in one of the newest additions to Abu Dhabi's five-star scene. Dine outside with views of the brightly coloured hotel dome, or

inside where you can watch the chefs prepare your curries from scratch. Each course is carefully constructed and the extensive menu proves that variety really is the spice of life. **Map** 1 H3

Aquarium
Seafood

Yas Marina, Yas Island
02 666 92220

One of the seven new or revamped restaurants to open up in the stylish Yas Marina, Aquarium delivers fresh seafood prepared in a no frills manner. Diners are greeted by the daily catch as they walk in, with fish tanks creating a cool back drop, although many choose to dine outside where the buzzing atmosphere and great views across the water to the Yas Viceroy make for a perfect setting. **Map** 1 H3

Arabesque
Buffet

Danat Al Ain Resort, Al Ain
03 704 6000

This top hotel buffet comes at a very affordable price. Served in spacious, attractive surroundings by polite and unobtrusive staff, the meal includes salads that are fresh and varied, and plenty of alternatives to the ubiquitous Lebanese mezze. Lunch is spiced up with a live cooking station and evenings include a small set menu that complements the buffet. The desserts are also worth a mention. **Map** 4 H8

Assymetri
European

Radisson Blu Hotel, Yas Island West
02 656 2000

Perfect for families with children, this restaurant is equipped with its own clown, toys and swimming pool. The international cuisine, by its very nature, caters for universal tastes and the live cooking stations make for dynamic entertainment. The large, bright interior also offers views over the Arabian Gulf and is a great spot for breakfast if staying at the hotel. **Map** 1 H3

Atayeb

Middle Eastern

Yas Viceroy Abu Dhabi, Yas Island West 02 656 0600

The clutch of awards adorning the entry to Atayeb speak volumes – Chef Wafaei, by many experts' reckoning, serves up the best Middle Eastern cuisine in Abu Dhabi. There are no real surprises – it's hot and cold mezze, grilled meat platters and grilled fish, and the dishes aren't too fussy and don't try too hard – but it's the quality that makes this restaurant stand out. If the season permits, Atayeb has one of the hotel's biggest terraces – ideal for smoking a relaxing post-meal shisha. **Map** 1 H3

BBQ Al Qasr

Emirati

Emirates Palace, Al Ras Al Akhdar 02 690 7999

High-quality chargrilled good, served on purpose-built pagoda platforms on Emirates Palace's own beach, this is barbecuing VIP style. The setting is perfect for a romantic evening with musicians playing chilled out tunes as you enjoy some excellent Arabic-inspired barbecue treats. Round off the evening with some shisha in this idyllic setting. **Map** 2 A2

Barouk

Middle Eastern

Crowne Plaza, Yas Island West 02 656 3000

This Lebanese restaurant is ideal for travellers wanting an authentic taste of the Middle East. With a wide selection of hot and cold mezze, sharing is advisable. Main course options are predominately a choice of juicy lamb or chicken kebabs. Sweeten things up with the exquisite Turkish delight – a perfect accompaniment to the restaurant's own belly dancer who makes an appearance late, transforming the atmosphere from quiet and refined to lively and vibrant. This is when it becomes more of a relaxed shisha bar too. **Map** 1 H3

Beach House

Mediterranean

Park Hyatt Hotel & Villas, Saadiyat Island

02 407 1138

The setting is beautiful, with palm trees and idyllic pools leading the way to the extremely sophisticated and picturesque restaurant on the beachfront. Ordering is a breeze thanks to the large menu full of delectable Mediterranean titbits. Much like a Spanish tapas bar, the idea here is to share dishes, and the fantastic array of little plates of deliciousness will make sure there's a taste for every palate. Since the restaurant is away from the bustle of the city, overlooking the waters of Saadiyat Beach, the Beach House makes for a great romantic spot, with the roof terrace an extra treat. **Map** 3 H2

Belgian Beer Cafe > *p.iv, 21*

Belgian

InterContinental Abu Dhabi, Al Bateen

02 666 6888

A lively, European-style cafe setting with lots of noise and laughter coming from the bar. Tuck into some of the best fries in the city, as well as pork cooked in a number of ways, but the specialty is steamed mussels. And it doesn't stop there – there are steaks, chicken and vegetarian selections to tantalise your taste buds. All this, and the extensive choice of beers, have made this a favourite among expats. **Map** 3 C4

Top: Chamas Churrascaria Restaurant & Bar; Bottom: Beach House

Benihana

Japanese

Beach Rotana, Tourist Club Area

02 697 9011

Contemporary Japanese cuisine, minimalist decor and crowd-pleasing teppanyaki chefs make this venue a must. The menu includes the usual soups, salads and desserts, but don't miss out on the sushi and, of course, the teppanyaki, prepared at live cooking stations. Prices may seem high but for a feast of melt-in-your-mouth treats, it's good value. **Map** 3 G4

Biancorosso Pizza

Italian

Y Tower, Nr Al Mamoura Bldg , Al Dhafra

02 658 4244

A pure pizzeria. The Italian owners have put a lot of effort into developing their signature dish, and the attention to detail pays off. It is quite possibly the best pizza in the capital, with crisp, light dough, a subtle hint of tomato sauce, and the perfect amount of fresh toppings. The menu also features traditional antipasti, salads, and pastas – well worth a sample, but the pizza is the focus and the delicious food and reasonable prices make it an eatery not to be missed. **Map** 1 F4

Blue Grill

Steakhouses

Yas Island Rotana, Yas Island West

02 656 4000

Elegant in shades of blue and dark wood, this restaurant, with its friendly and attentive staff, is light and airy. There's an extensive range of wine and an impressive show kitchen. Monday to Thursday, the restaurant offers an innovative a la carte menu, focusing on prime beef and seafood and, on Fridays, it hosts a truly sumptuous brunch that's a popular establishment among residents. **Map** 1 H3

Bord Eau

French

Shangri-La Hotel, Qaryat Al Beri, Al Maqtaa 02 509 8511

Chef Gilles Perrin produces some gastronomic masterpieces, and the menu takes established luxuries – foie gras, scallops, lobster Thermidor and Wagyu beef – and adds subtle twists. There is a hushed air of fine dining, and people come here for special occasions or for business meetings. The service is faultless, but dinner for two will leave a considerable hole in your wallet. One of Abu Dhabi's finest. **Map** 2 D2

Casa Romana Restaurant

Italian

Hilton Al Ain, Al Ain 03 768 6666

The well-known Italian joint Casa Romana overlooks the bustling lobby of the hotel, and has an extensive menu of authentic Italian dishes, all generously portioned and delicious. You'll find all-Italian favourites from pizza and pasta to seafood risotto here. The decor evokes the feel of a rustic country terrace. **Map** 4 G8

Chamas Churrascaria & Bar > *p.iv, 21*

Brazilian

InterContinental, Al Bateen 02 666 6888

The concept is simple – all the red meat you can eat for a fixed price. The meat is fantastic and the salad bar is large enough to appease any vegetarians you may be dining with. All of it is included in the price. Be careful when ordering, however, as drinks and desserts aren't included. This noisy, frantic place, with its enthusiastic band, is great for large groups and is packed every night, proving that Chamas has got the formula for Brazilian churrascaria just right. **Map** 3 A3

Cho Gao
Asian

Crowne Plaza, Markaziya East
02 616 6166

Cho Gao's menu reads like a food travelogue – an ingredient from China, a recipe from Thailand, a technique from Vietnam; salad, soup, dim sum. Recommended are the steak, duck and seafood options, while you'll also find some of the most creative vegetarian dishes in town. The ambience is calm and the decor authentic, while the service is attentive without being intrusive and the bar, with its two-for-one happy hour, is great for a quick drink and a snack after work. **Map** 3 F3

Diablito
Mediterranean

Yas Marina, Yas Island
050 917 5605

One of the six new or revamped restaurants at the stylish Yas Marina, Diablito is probably the most laid back with no real dress code. Take to the rooftop of this simple yet effective venue and enjoy excellent pizza or a range of authentic tapas. Prices are reasonable, the music good and the atmosphere will have you thinking you're dining out in a totally different continent. A free Yas Express bus runs to the marina from all of the island's hotels, so it really is a must-visit. **Map** 1 H3

El Sombrero
Mexican

Sheraton Hotel & Resort,
Markaziya East
02 697 0224

Whether you're out for a relaxed dinner for two or are starting out on a raucous night with your amigos, El Sombrero delivers on all fronts. Fascinating Mexican artefacts and well thought-out decor set the scene, while the Tex-Mex themed cuisine and the friendly, fun service both score highly as well to create a local Markaziya favourite. The atmosphere is lively, so this is a reasonable bet on most nights of the week, while booking may be necessary at weekends. **Map** 3 F2

Filini

Italian

Radisson Blu Hotel, Yas Island West 02 656 2000

A spacious, modern restaurant where warming beiges, creams and dark woods calm the senses; if the weather allows, the terrace is an equally peaceful and charming dining space with views across the golf course and over the water. Filini unashamedly wears its Italian heart on its sleeve, and the classic selection of pizza, fish, meat and pasta is done very well, especially the steak. The wine, service and presentation are all excellent while the bar is also perfect for a quiet chat over a deep claret. **Map** 1 H3

Finz

Seafood

Beach Rotana, Tourist Club Area 02 697 9011

Sitting well apart from the other restaurants at the Beach Rotana, patrons might get the feeling that they're on something of a seafood pilgrimage upon arriving at Finz. The restaurant's ample menu doesn't disappoint – from lobster to sea bass, and huge king prawns, this place will keep you salivating. It's not cheap, but it's worth it for the oysters on the half shell alone. Attentive service and a gorgeous terrace setting (though sometimes marred by the construction on Sowwah Island) can turn a simple meal into a dining experience worthy of any holiday. **Map** 3 G4

Fishmarket > *p.iv, 21*

Seafood

InterContinental, Al Bateen

02 666 6888

With the tropical island decor and the smiley service, diners will immediately realise this is no business-as-usual Abu Dhabi hotel restaurant. From extensive selection of fresh seafood, as well as a cartload of fresh vegetables, noodles and rice, customers choose the style of cooking (grilled, sauteed, fried); the kind of sauce (green curry, red curry, oyster sauce); and the accompaniments. **Map** 3 A3

Frankie's Italian Restaurant & Bar

Italian

Fairmont Bab Al Bahr, Al Maqtaa

02 654 3238

This is world-class dining in a chic, romantic setting. Attention to detail is key, from the eclectic decor, mouth-watering menu and outstanding service, right down to the lighting. Diners can feast on the freshest Italian fare, ranging from home-made pastas and wood-fired pizzas, to gourmet treats like grilled Canadian lobster and beef tenderloin. **Map** 2 D1

The Garden Restaurant

International

Crowne Plaza, Markaziya East

02 616 6166

This faux alfresco 'garden' venue is decorated with an abundance of plants and even has a waterfall. Theme nights cover the cuisines of the world, and every evening you'll find an impressive buffet designed to delight your taste buds. The Friday brunch is a popular family affair, with tasty food and plenty of entertainment for the kids, so you can enjoy a long lunch with a variety of liquid refreshments. **Map** 3 F3

Clockwise from top left: The Garden Restaurant, Hakkasan, Cho Gao

Gerard Patisserie

Cafes & Coffee Shops
Marina Mall, Breakwater
02 681 4642

Located at the top of the escalators in the popular Marina Mall, Gerard's is a great venue for a spot of people watching or a quick pit stop during an energy-sapping shopping spree. The simple menu offers light meals, soups and sandwiches, and of course there is a good selection of pastries and both hot and cold beverages. **Map** 3 B1

Hakkasan

Far Eastern
Emirates Palace, Al Ras Al Akhdar
02 690 7999

An offshoot of the legendary establishment in London, Hakkasan's Abu Dhabi location has become arguably the hottest dining address in town since its opening in 2010. The setting in Emirates Palace is stunning and the food is in a league of its own when it comes to oriental fusion cuisine; everything is made with the freshest of ingredients and it's a restaurant that is best enjoyed by ordering plenty to share and then all diving in. **Map** 3 A2

Havana Cafe

Cafes & Coffee Shops
Nr Marina Mall, Hamdan St, Breakwater
02 681 0044

Situated in one of the finest locations in Abu Dhabi, Havana Cafe has stunning views that encourage relaxed alfresco dining. The menu is international, and while breakfast and lunch are fairly quiet affairs, Havana later transforms into a vibrant dinner venue. The service is courteous, and a 'shisha man' in traditional costume is an added attraction.
Map 3 B1

Heroes
American

Crowne Plaza, Markaziya East 02 616 6166

One of the city's best sports bars, Heroes often heaves with frenzied fans who come to watch the game in the company of similarly sports-mad folk. The pub fare is tasty and portions are generous. Thankfully, the table service is friendly and surprisingly efficient, so there is no need to wrestle through the crowds to get to the bar. Regular events such as Ladies Night, Quiz Night and Dance Night pack in the punters. **Map** 3 F3

Hoi An
Vietnamese

Shangri-La Hotel, Qaryat Al Beri, Al Maqtaa 02 509 8888

The comprehensive menu comprises traditional Vietnamese favourites and delicious originals, such as kobe steak in a rich foie gras sauce. Subtly decorated in a far eastern style indoors, the outdoor tables overlook the Al Maqtaa area and offer a more secluded dining experience. **Map** 2 D2

Il Porto
Italian

Mirage Marine Complex, Nr Marina Mall, Breakwater 02 635 9957

The restaurant features a stylish interior that is eclipsed by the outdoor terrace with views over the pristine blue waters to Emirates Palace. On offer is an intriguing mix of contemporary Italian fare and sushi to create a contemporary dining experience (the menu combination feels a little peculiar, but it works nicely). The service is simple and gracious, and the dishes mouth-watering, but the restaurant is further elevated by its location. **Map** 3 B1

India Palace
Indian

Nr ADNOC, Al Salam St, Tourist Club Area 02 644 8777

This unassuming restaurant features an extensive menu, and a buzzing atmosphere. The food is tasty and at times pretty fiery, and portions are generous, offering good value for your dirham. Those with more delicate palates can request milder versions of their favourites. Quick, courteous waiters will patiently guide you through the menu if you are not an expert on North Indian cuisine. **Map** 3 F3

Jing Asia
Asian

Crowne Plaza, Yas Island West 02 656 3000

Contemporary and colourful on the inside, with a rejuvenating sea view from the outside areas, the ambience at Jing Asia is impressive either way. Attentive, friendly staff prepare fresh ingredients in the open kitchen. The menu features traditional Asian cuisine from sushi to stir fries; Friday brunch casts the net wider, even boasting a traditional roast with Yorkshire pudding. Ideal for large groups or parties, there are a variety of themed nights throughout the week. **Map** 1 H3

Kazu
Japanese

Yas Viceroy, Yas Island West 02 656 0600

The interior is simple, modern and nicely lit, and the terrace overlooking the Yas Marina and the race circuit makes for a unique backdrop to a social restaurant. Head chef Yu Cao trained under Nobu Matsuhisa, but it's possible that he has eclipsed his master's Dubai offering. The exceptional lightness and clarity of flavours almost defies belief, with the cucumber

Jing Asia

and seafood salad, shrimp and cream cheese sushi and teppanyaki particularly special. Often rated as one of the best Japanese restaurants in town. **Map** 1 H3

Kwality

Indian

Nr National Bank of Fujairah, Al Salam St, Markaziya East — 02 672 7337

If you like authentic Indian food at a very reasonable price, then Kwality is one of the best options in town. From North Indian tandoori dishes to Goan curries, Kwality provides a wonderful tour through Indian cuisine. The food, service, and welcoming atmosphere make this one of the 'must do' Indian restaurants in the capital. **Map** 3 G2

La Mamma

Italian

Sheraton Hotel & Resort, Markaziya East — 02 697 0224

This spacious, well-appointed restaurant is an excellent choice for a romantic evening, a fun family feast or a respectable business meal. With the exception of the exotic antipasto buffet, the food is fairly standard but is well prepared and of good quality, from quick and filling pizzas to delicious and generous helpings of pasta and seafood. **Map** 3 E2

Le Beaujolais

French

Mercure Abu Dhabi Centre Hotel, Markaziya East — 02 633 3555

With its red-checked tablecloths and French-speaking, glass-clinking clientele, Le Beaujolais virtually transports you to a charming little bistro in Paris. The menu offers seafood and meat dishes, rounded off with a dessert selection including crackly crusted creme brulee. A daily set menu is also available. The service, headed by a friendly maitre d', is welcoming and attentive, but never obtrusive. **Map** 3 E2

Le Bistrot

French

Le Meridien, Tourist Club Area

02 644 6666

Connoisseurs of fine wines and elegant French cuisine will enjoy a superb culinary experience at Le Bistrot in Le Meridien. In cooler months, the terrace offers a great opportunity to people watch while feasting on some top quality fare. The menu is a little limited but fans of simple fish and meat dishes prepared in a classic French style will be more than happy. Cheap it isn't, but you get what you pay for. **Map** 3 G3

Le Boulanger

Cafes & Coffee Shops

BHS Bldg, Shk Hamdan Bin Mohd St, Markaziya East — 02 631 8115

This busy French cafe in the heart of the city is a great place to enjoy a European style breakfast, good coffee and a leisurely browse through the daily newspapers from around the world. The menu is extensive, featuring tasty food in generous quantities. There is a bakery counter selling the freshest breads, croissants, tarts and cakes, which can be eaten on the premises or taken home to enjoy later (or both). **Map** 3 F3

Lebanese Flower

Middle Eastern

Nr Shk Zayed The First & Al Nahyan Sts, Al Khalidiyah — 02 665 8700

This popular restaurant has a range of high quality grilled meats and fish accompanied by delicious freshly baked Arabic bread. A selection of Middle Eastern curries and meat dishes are available at lunchtime. Service is super efficient – the slightest nod of your head will instantly bring a bevy of enthusiastic waiters to your table. **Map** 3 C3

Li Beirut

Lebanese

Jumeirah At Etihad Towers Al Ras Al Akhdar — 02 811 5666

A fine-looking restaurant, modern and elegant, bright white table clothes teamed with deep red chairs and dark wooden finishes. On the terrace, views over the pool provide a wow factor you may not expect. It's most accurate to describe Li Beirut as a European restaurant that uses Lebanese flavours. Traditional breads and mezze are creatively reinvented as interesting and yummy starters, while the main courses are focused on great cuts of meat and fish. The honey fudge dessert has gained something of a reputation for being one of the city's tastiest indulgences. **Map** 3 A2

Marco Pierre White Steakhouse & Grill

Steakhouses

Fairmont Bab Al Bahr, Al Maqtaa

02 654 3238

This beautifully appointed restaurant delivers contemporary British food, elevated to delicious standards. Although the restaurant is named after its celeb chef founder, take just one bite into the pepper sauce topped fillet and you'll know this is a restaurant that could never be accused of being style over substance. It's a dinner only restaurant (ie. not open for lunch) but you could easily spend the whole evening here. **Map** 2 D1

Mawal

Middle Eastern

Hilton Abu Dhabi, Al Khubeirah

02 681 1900

An Arabian belly dancer and singer top the bill at Mawal, but the excellent food, colourful service and lively atmosphere are enough draw in themselves. In addition to an exhaustive range of hot and cold Lebanese mezze, is a selection of superb kebabs grilled to perfection, including a melting lamb shish. If you plan to stay for the show, reservations are essential as the place really comes alive later on. Although it is a bit pricey, this restaurant is worth every dirham for a Lebanese banquet and a full night's Arabian entertainment. **Map** 3 A2

The Meat Co

Steakhouses

Souk Qaryat Al Beri, Al Maqtaa
02 558 1713

The Meat Co is a large restaurant, covering two floors plus a big outdoor deck. The energy of the open kitchen spills out to the restaurant, giving the place a frenetic atmosphere, which makes it a popular choice for groups. The service is ok, but the meat is by far the best reason for coming here. The beef menu is extensive, and the tempting flavours alone, lingering from the open kitchen, whet the appetite. **Map** 2 D1

Mezzaluna

Italian

Emirates Palace, Al Ras Al Akhdar
02 690 7999

From the time the complimentary breads and olives are placed in front of you, until the time you devour the last crumb of your wicked (but wonderful) dessert, your experience at Mezzaluna will be a guaranteed delight. The Italian head chef uses divine inspiration to create a host of beautifully presented dishes, including fresh pasta concoctions, seafood creations and meat dishes, many of which are surprisingly easy on the pocket. Stunning decor and an opulent atmosphere also please, and the terrace tables grant wonderful views of the hotel's stunning beach area. **Map** 3 A2

Min Zaman

Middle Eastern

Al Ain Rotana, Al Ain
03 754 5111

Once you manage to find this restaurant in the depths of the Al Ain Rotana hotel (ask for directions at reception), you are in for a superb evening of regional food and entertainment.

Clockwise from top left: Porto Bello, Le Boulanger, Ornina

WEDDING CAKE
BAPTISMAL CAKE
BIRTHDAY CAKE
NESCAFE

Hot and cold mezze head the menu, followed by the usual array of grilled meats and fish, while desserts and shisha are all enjoyed against a backdrop of live music, singing and belly dancing. It can get crowded on Thursday nights, so reservations are recommended. **Map** 4 G8

Nihal Restaurant

Indian

Nr Sands Hotel, Shk Zayed The Second St, Madinat Zayed

02 631 8088

This established Indian restaurant offers great curries at rock bottom prices, and the menu is extensive enough to tickle just about anyone's fancy. The fragrant spices of the subcontinent are all expertly blended into tasty traditional dishes, served up with the usual relishes, yoghurts and chutneys. And even if Indian food is not your favourite, there is another option; the restaurant serves, rather peculiarly, some Chinese dishes too. **Map** 3 F3

Nolu's

Cafes & Coffee Shops

Al Bandar, Al Raha

02 557 9500

Inspired by Afghani cuisine and California recipes, this laid back cafe at the Al Bandar complex has a special menu for kids but is definitely a treat for all the family. From chocolate drenched French toast to salmon kebabs and make-your-own salads, it's great for any meal of the day. In fact, even the side salads are so large just one could last you for a couple of meals. The decor is fun, with views out of the side windows of the water, and its reputation is growing all of the time. Rumours are that royalty is even amongst its fans. **Map** 1 H3

Noodle Box

Contemporary Asian

Yas Viceroy, Yas Island West 02 656 0600

Noodle Box is a chic, romantic venue with an outdoor terrace overlooking the Yas Marina and F1 track. The simple menu features pan-Asian favourites from prawn cakes prepared with fresh chillies and lime leaves to signature dim sum and wok specialties, all cooked with the freshest ingredients, although some dishes can be quite heavy on the seasoning. The wine list and the house specialty beer, Tsingtao, complement the cuisine. **Map** 1 H3

THE One

Cafes & Coffee Shops

Khalidiya Theatre & Restaurant, Shk Zayed The First St, Al Khalidiyah 02 681 6500

With soft lighting and smart furnishings, this cafe echoes the shop in which it's situated. There are three distinct menus depending on your mood: the 'Chic' menu is crammed with healthy options, 'Vogue' features traditional dishes including soups and salads, and 'Risque' is home to familiar dishes with an unexpected twist, such as Mexican falafel. Vegetarians will be particularly pleased with the selection on offer. **Map** 3 B3

Ornina

Mediterranean

Al Bandar Marina Al Raha Beach 02 556 6090

A unique proposition, Ornina is a licensed bar-restaurant at the Al Bandar residential complex and marina in Al Raha Beach. The stunning wooden-clad exterior is matched by an equally stylish Scandinavian-inspired interior with impressive views across the water to Yas Island. Food is Mediterranean with a twist, with delicious tastes of Spain flowing through the tapas. It's also a popular spot for going out, with a fantastic outside area for some sophisticated food and drinks. Regular theme nights make means almost every night serves up some **Map** 1 H3

Pachaylen

Thai

Eastern Mangroves Hotel & Spa by Anantara, Al Matar

02 656 1000

Pachaylen is a full-on embrace of Anantara's Thai heritage, from the all-Thai kitchen and waiting-on staff to the menu. You'll be hard-pressed to find a more beautifully decked-out restaurant in Abu Dhabi. The soft shell crab salad is the stand-out starter, while you should look no further than the slow-cooked Thai curries for main course. This is a long way from traditional street food and the spiciness isn't overdone either. The banana pancake spring rolls or sticky rice and fruit are the perfect ways to finish. **Map** 1 D3

Palm Lounge

Cafes & Coffee Shops

Le Royal Meridien, Markaziya East

02 674 2020

The timeless (and very British) tradition of afternoon tea is perfectly executed here, with dainty finger sandwiches and fresh, plump scones served on fine bone china plates, while you gaze out over the beautiful gardens and the pianist plays softly in the background. If you wish to indulge, upgrade to the Royal traditional tea which includes a glass of chilled champagne. **Map** 3 F2

Pappagallo

Italian

Le Meridien, Tourist Club Area — 02 644 6666

Pappagallo is like a little slice of Tuscany right in the heart of the Le Meridien Culinary Village. The menu caters to most tastes, offering all the usual favourites from pastas to pizzas, as well as a wonderful antipasti buffet. Whether you dine alfresco or indoors, the atmosphere is pleasant. **Map** 3 G3

The Park Bar & Grill

Steakhouses

Park Hyatt Hotel & Villas, Saadiyat Island — 02 407 1138

Spread over two levels, with an effortlessly chic speakeasy serving up cocktails, scotches, cognacs and cigars on the upper level, and a modern, classy restaurant with poolside terrace on the lower level, The Park Bar & Grill is a venue that would grace anywhere from New York to Nice. The restaurant is spacious but well laid-out and creatively-lit to create a feeling of intimacy. Food is generally high-end bistro fare, with charcoal-grilled meats and fish at the top of the menu, although Asian flavours add a nice twist. **Map** 1 D1

Pearls & Caviar

Seafood

Shangri-La Hotel, Qaryat Al Beri, Al Maqtaa — 02 509 8777

Inside this posh restaurant is a sleek world of black, white and chrome. Outside, one of the most inspiring views of the Sheikh Zayed Grand Mosque can be admired shimmering in the waters of the creek. The extensive menu offers a splendid seafood selection, including plenty of caviar. Prices and service reflect the luxury menu items, and dinner for two will set you back around Dhs.1,200. **Map** 2 D2

Porto Bello
Italian

Grand Millennium Al Wahda, Al Dhafra
02 443 9999

Whether you dine in the spacious restaurant (where a pianist and cellist provide background music) or opt for the atmospheric terrace area, the food is first class Italian, with a good selection of dishes. The signature lasagna is a fine example of the elegant cooking style, as are the smoked duck risotto and osso buco Milanese. Top choice. **Map** 3 E5

Prego's
Italian

Beach Rotana, Tourist Club Area
02 697 9011

Prego's boasts a large, airy interior and superb terrace overlooking the beach. The food is wonderful – in addition to the pizzas prepared in an authentic wood-fired oven, the menu has a selection of both classic and innovative pasta dishes, main courses and desserts. The venue is family friendly. **Map** 3 G4

Quest
Asian

Jumeirah at Etihad Towers, Al Ras Al Akhdar
02 811 5666

The restaurant is beautiful and elegant – all tables offer incredible views from the 63rd floor as well as being spread around the open kitchen. But, as Abu Dhabi sparkles below, it's the service – just about perfect – and the food that captures the attention. Officially, it's Pan-Asian fare, but this is the kind of Cantonese or Malaysian food that Heston Blumenthal or Ferran Adria might serve up – deconstructed and reinterpreted, it's never pretentious but intriguing, fun and downright tasty. It's an exciting and innovative experience. **Map** 3 A2

Clockwise from top left: Spaccanapoli Fistorante, Shang Palace, Prego's

Rangoli
Indian

Yas Island Rotana, Yas Island West
02 656 4000

Rangoli's laidback vibe provides the perfect setting for its delicious buffet serving North and South Indian cuisine that is fresh and attractive. Starters and mains intermingle; vegetable samosas and home-made chutneys sitting beside meat, fish and vegetable curries. Sweet lovers can choose from traditional desserts, including milky payas, sticky laddu, and exotic fruits. With a la carte options available and friendly staff, Rangoli offers a good value curry fix. **Map** 1 H3

Riviera
Cafes & Coffee Shops

Nr Abu Dhabi Post Office, Tourist Club Area
02 676 6615

This bright and airy cafe mixes a relaxed Mediterranean setting with typical Lebanese cuisine. The tasty mezze and freshly grilled dishes are recommended, and accompanied perfectly by piping hot Arabic bread which is baked on the premises. You'll even find a few European specialities on the menu, just in case Lebanese food doesn't tickle your fancy. **Map** 3 G3

Rock Bottom Cafe
American

Al Diar Capital Hotel, Tourist Club Area
02 678 7700

Named after the Wall Street crash, this vibrant American diner has a somewhat split personality – go early in the evening to enjoy a quiet dinner, or hang around until later when the live music starts and the pace becomes frenetic. The menu features succulent steaks, sizzling seafood and innovative salads, as well as a range of lighter snacks. **Map** 3 G2

Rodeo Grill

Steakhouses

Beach Rotana, Tourist Club Area — 02 697 9011

Part old English drawing room, part old American shooting lodge, Rodeo Grill comes across as a high-end Argentinean ranch. Salads, seafood and even a few veggie options make it on to the menu, but the spotlight shines firmly on the fantastic range of steak cuts, with the grade nine marble Wagyu and the bison rib eye the stars of the show. Prices are certainly not cheap, but this is a truly excellent restaurant. **Map** 3 G4

Sevilla

International

Al Raha Beach Hotel, Al Raha — 02 508 0555

Offering both a la carte and buffet dishes, the food is excellent and the overall experience is complemented by efficient and friendly service. The buffet options are available on Wednesdays, Thursdays and at Friday brunch. The beautifully decorated ceilings add a special touch to the warm, intimate interior, though for a stunning view, opt for a table on the terrace. **Map** 1 G4

Shang Palace

Chinese

Shangri-La Hotel, Qaryat Al Beri, Al Maqtaa — 02 509 8503

Shang Palace's extensive menu covers Cantonese and Szechuan cuisine in addition to many non-Chinese items, and seafood features prominently. The atmosphere is great, the service faultless, the staff impeccably dressed, and the food superb. The breath-taking views from the romantic terrace are more than enough reason to come and linger for the evening in the large, solid chairs. **Map** 2 D2

Sofra Bld

International

Shangri-La Hotel, Qaryat Al Beri, Al Maqtaa 02 509 8555

Any restaurant that can boast three chocolate fountains is worth a visit. Accompanying the fountains is a breathtaking array of intricate buffet cuisine covering all four corners of the globe, from fresh sushi to shawarma kebabs and parrot fish. The light and airy interior is less suited to intimate occasions, while the outside terrace provides a perfect vantage point for views of the neighbouring Sheikh Zayed Grand Mosque. **Map** 2 D2

Spaccanapoli Ristorante

Italian

Crowne Plaza, Markaziya East 02 616 6166

This Italian restaurant is focused squarely on Naples and, although thoroughly modern, it has plenty of rustic features which embrace the traditional quality of simple Italian fare. Treats such as baked aubergine with mozzarella get the meal off to an excellent start, and all the traditional main courses are represented. Try the veal escalope, the fresh fish or, if you're hungry, the metre-long pizza with up to four toppings. The food is excellent, the prices reasonable and it is suitable for a romantic dinner or a livelier affair. **Map** 3 F3

Tanjore

Indian

Danat Al Ain Resort, Al Ain 03 704 6000

Tanjore is a curry lover's dream. The menu is varied enough to please the most demanding of tastes, and provides clear descriptions on what's hot, hotter, healthy and vegetarian. The atmosphere and surroundings complement the delicious and tantalising flavours, and the service is good. **Map** 4 G8

Clockwise from top left: Trader Vic's, The Wok, The Meat Co

Teatro
Fusion

Park Rotana Abu Dhabi, Al Matar
02 657 3333

Teatro's eclectic decor creates a dramatic but informal atmosphere which is echoed by the huge show kitchen. Choose from an impressive a la carte menu, which covers a spectrum of east to west fine dining dishes honed in Teatro's very popular Dubai restaurant. Service is absolutely impeccable and the whole Teatro experience is fast becoming a firm favourite among residents and tourists. **Map** 2 C1

Trader Vic's
Polynesian

Al Ain Rotana, Al Ain
03 754 5111

Forget the desert and spend an evening in full Hawaiian shirt tropical island mode at this popular Polynesian venue. The menu may forgo authentic Polynesian food, preferring instead to satisfy the cosmopolitan clientele with a delicious and diverse range of international dishes, but the atmosphere is lively (Polynesian-style bands often provide the dancing tunes) and the creatively delivered cocktails are so potent they should probably carry a health warning. **Map** 4 G8

Trader Vic's
Polynesian

Beach Rotana, Tourist Club Area
02 697 9011

Whether for business or pleasure, Trader Vic's is one of Abu Dhabi's long-standing favourite restaurants. The consistent quality of the food, the attentive staff and the relaxed tropical ambience keep people coming back time and time again. Try one of their world-famous cocktails as you peruse the exciting menu of tantalising French Polynesian dishes. **Map** 3 G4

Ushna

Indian

Souk Qaryat Al Beri, Al Maqtaa — 02 558 1769

Ushna's sophisticated surroundings complement the beautifully prepared food. During the cooler months, grab a table by the water overlooking the Grand Mosque. There is a varied selection of traditional North Indian dishes and delicately spiced curries to choose from. On the drinks-front, you get to choose from a large range of premium wines and a great cocktail list. All in all, Ushna is a great place for a relaxed and enjoyable evening out. **Map** 2 D1

Vasco's

Portuguese

Hilton Abu Dhabi, Al Khubeirah — 02 681 1900

Vasco's is a contemporary, fine dining venue offering a fusion of European, Arabic and Asian cuisines. Food is prepared to a very high standard and imaginatively presented. The patio offers a pleasant, alfresco setting, and as this is one of the more popular restaurants in Abu Dhabi, reservations are recommended whether for lunch or dinner. **Map** 3 A2

The Village Club

International

One To One Hotel – The Village, Al Dhafra — 02 495 2000

The Village Club is situated amid a mature lawn with huge trees and scattered with tables and comfortable Arabic tents. At the buffet, starters include soup, mezze and salads. From the barbecue, there's a variety of beef, lamb, chicken and fish, along with side dishes. Weekends are great for families, and in the evenings it is a relaxing place to enjoy a calmer meal along with shisha or drinks. **Map** 3 F6

Wasabi

Japanese
Al Diar Mina Hotel, Al Meena
02 678 1000

Enter the stark minimalism of the Wasabi interior for a light, healthy twist on Japanese cuisine – think fusion rather than authentic Japanese. The appetisers, including chicken dumplings, sushi and sashimi, are good value for money and are light enough to pave the way for a main course dish such as black bean noodles or teriyaki smoked salmon. In addition to conventional wine, there's a good range of Japanese sake, served hot or cold. **Map** 3 G2

The Wok

Far Eastern
Danat Al Ain Resort, Al Ain
03 704 6000

Staff members here are proud of their food, service and reputation, and with good reason – The Wok is one of the better restaurants serving Far Eastern cuisine in the area. Set in the landscaped grounds of the hotel, the ambience is quiet and relaxed with soft background music and stylish decor. The Wok is popular and reservations are essential, particularly for the outstanding seafood buffet on Sunday nights.
Map 4 H8

Zest

International
Al Ain Rotana, Al Ain
03 754 5111

A carved ice swan presides over an array of fresh seafood laid out in a wooden dhow to set the mood. Previously known as Gardinia, this venue is popular throughout the week and reservations are recommended. Seafood lovers won't know where to start with the amazing choice, but the seafood

Teatro

chowder is among the recommended dishes, along with the red snapper. As for the desserts, if you have room then you won't be disappointed. **Map** 4 G8

Zyara Cafe

Cafes & Coffee Shops

Nr Corniche Residence, East Corniche St, Al Khalidiyah

02 627 5007

Zyara in Arabic means 'visit' and this trendy cafe definitely deserves one. The glass frontage offers a good view of the Corniche, and the laidback interior, with its rustic, Victorian style is an ideal meeting place. The quality and presentation of the food is excellent and the service is friendly and attentive. All this does come at a price, though. **Map** 3 D1

Bars, Pubs & Clubs

There are a decent number of bars and clubs on offer in the city, which range from uber-trendy cocktail lounges to jazz, cigar and champagne bars.

Captain's Arms

Bars

Le Meridien, Tourist Club Area 02 644 6666

Overlooking the gardens of Le Meridien, this tavern, with its cosy interior, offers the ambience of a traditional British pub. But unlike at UK boozers, the lively terrace is the perfect place to enjoy chilled-out drinks and chat throughout most of the year. The daily happy hour (18:00 to 20:00), nightly entertainment, and food and drink specials bring in the crowds throughout the week. Food portions are generous and generally satisfying, although you won't find many culinary surprises here. **Map** 3 G3

Cloud Nine – Cigar & Champagne Bar

Cigar Bars

Sheraton Hotel & Resort,
Markaziya East 02 677 3333

From the first puff on your hand-picked Cohiba, Monte Cristo or Bolivar (delivered to you on a silver platter), to the last bit of Beluga passing your lips, this luxurious venue exudes a pleasing mix of old boys' charm and trendy sophistication. Service is pleasant and discreet, and a pianist adds further elegance to a classy (albeit smoky) evening out. **Map** 3 F2

Cooper's Bar & Restaurant

Pubs

Park Rotana, Al Matar

02 657 3333

Cooper's is among the favourite hangouts for Abu Dhabi expats. Not only will you find a friendly pint and some superb pub grub, but all major football matches are also shown here (call ahead for details). Cooper's offers 50% off selected beverages during its extended happy hour. With its spacious interior and additional seating outside, it's great for informal gatherings. **Map** 2 C1

Cristal

Cigar Bars

Millennium Hotel, Markaziya East

02 614 6020

Once the masterful bar manager has poured you a glass of champagne and helped you select the perfect smoke, you can sit back and relax in surroundings of polished wood, leather and subdued lighting. The tinkling tunes played by the in-house pianist make the perfect accompaniment, and if all this sophistication leaves you feeling peckish, a small range of tasty snacks is available. **Map** 3 F2

Havana Club

Bars

Emirates Palace, Al Ras Al Akhdar

02 690 7999

In keeping with the grandeur of the hotel, the Havana Club exudes opulence and luxury while hinting at the personality of an 'old boys club' type exclusive bar. The bar area has a younger, more outgoing spirit, while the deep leather armchairs tucked in at the back are the personification of refinement. Relax and enjoy an exotic cocktail or maybe a vintage brandy, and snack on exquisitely presented canapes.

You can even enjoy a fine Cuban cigar or cigarillo. The Havana club is open from 18:00 to 02:00 daily. **Map** 3 A2

Hickory's Sports Bar

Sports Bars

Yas Links, Yas Island West — 02 810 7710

Hickory's is a sports bar, but that title doesn't really do it justice. Sure, major sporting events and news adorn the large plasma screens, but the feel is of a private members' club; the robust menu of wood-fired pizzas, huge pies and steaks is also a cut above. For something different, try the tasty tapas style snacks on the terrace and soak up the amazing views. **Map** 1 H3

The Jazz Bar & Dining

Jazz Bars

Hilton Abu Dhabi, Al Khubeirah — 02 681 1900

For a relaxed evening of jazz, champagne and good food in a stylish setting, the Jazz Bar is worth a visit. Each dish on the extensive menu is available in two sizes – 'down beat' for the not so hungry, and 'main melody' for the ravenous. Special dietary needs can be met on request. As can be expected in any good bar, the wine list and drinks selection are impressive. The popular band keeps the rhythm alive and attracts a crowd, especially at weekends. **Map** 3 A2

Lemon & Lime

Cigar & Wine Bars

Westin Golf Resort & Spa, Khalifa City — 02 616 9999

An elegant wine and cigar bar, Lemon & Lime is the kind of place you can start your night at, or just spend the whole evening soaking up the chic atmosphere. The decor is contemporary luxury, although the amazing golf course views dominate. There are some delicious snacks available, and the variety of wines on offer is exceptional. **Map** 1 F4

O1NE Yas Island

Nightclubs

Yas Island West

052 788 8111

The graffiti-clad cylindrical nightclub opened up just in time for the 2013 Formula 1 Grand Prix and did so with a bang. Celebrity acts frequent this exclusive venue, with the city's clubbing elite making it a regular Thursday evening outing. Open until the last dancer can handle no more, O1NE Yas Island is the club to be seen at. **Map** 1 H3

Paco's
Sports Bars
Hilton Al Ain, Al Ain
03 768 6666

Paco's has become somewhat of a living legend thanks to the fact that it never changes. Popular because it is exactly the same now as it was when it opened in 1991, this British watering hole is a tonic for the homesick expat's soul. After a steaming plate of bangers and mash, an excellent pint of Guinness (hard to come by in these parts of the world) and a spot of footie on the big screen, you'll almost forget you are not back in England. There's a daily happy hour between 16:00 and 19:00. **Map** 4 H8

PJ O'Reilly's
Pubs
Le Royal Meridien, Markaziya East
02 674 2020

This Irish pub is extremely popular, with a friendly and inviting atmosphere. The menu is pub grub with flair, with large portions and good value for money. The lively bar downstairs is the place to meet and greet, though you can escape to the quieter upstairs or alfresco dining areas. Big-screen TVs show sport, but the sound is generally only on during live football matches. Happy hour runs from 12:00 to 19:00 every day, with other specials happening regularly through the week. **Map** 3 F2

Relax@12
Bars
Aloft, Al Safarat
02 654 5183

Whether in the mood for after-work cocktails in the rooftop lounge or a casual meal alfresco, this spot hits the mark. The decor is decidedly modern with glowing bars, dim lighting and angular furniture, but both the terrace and the bar attract a refreshing mix of ages. The view alone is worth a visit, but with an extensive menu of beer, wine and cocktails, and a small but dependable menu of sushi and Japanese favourites, this is a perfect spot for making a night of it. **Map** 2 A2

SAX

Jazz Bars

Le Royal Meridien, Markaziya East

02 674 2020

The chic set will love this restaurant's trendy, New York style. A live jazz band and a well-stocked bar contribute to the vibey atmosphere as you unwind on the comfortable sofas with one of the many exotic cocktails on offer. Like most trendy

eateries, the quality of the ingredients and presentation cannot be faulted, and special drink offers and free cocktails for ladies help to make the evening even more enjoyable. **Map** 3 F2

Stills Bar & Brasserie

Bars

Crowne Plaza, Yas Island West — 02 656 3000

This lively bar serves the cool youth as well as the gracefully aged. There's a nice list of specialty cocktails and whisky, as well as several international beers on tap and a cigar humidor giving the impression that this bar is serious about fun. The gastro-pub menu serves everything from steaks and burgers to pan-seared salmon, while the picturesque terrace is perfect for the mild breezy nights. There's also a DJ pool party night once a month, and Stills serves as a sometime-stopover for touring bands. **Map** 1 H3

Y Bar

Bars

Yas Island Rotana, Yas Island West — 02 656 4000

Sit inside the cellar-styled Y Bar's long wooden tables and watch sport on TV or, if the weather permits, choose the outside terrace which has ambient lighting, low seating, and overlooks the other Yas hotels. The extensive drinks menu focuses on cocktails and spirits with a decent list of beers and wine. The food menu, although small, provides tasty basics such as shepherd's pie, and steak and chips along with a handful of bar snacks. Reggae tunes help to give the bar an informal atmosphere, with friendly staff helping to give some residents that feeling of having a traditional 'local'. **Map** 1 H3

Index

#

A

explorer

Explorer Products

Check out ask**explorer**.com/shop

Residents' Guides

Visitors' Guides

Photography Books & Calendars

Maps

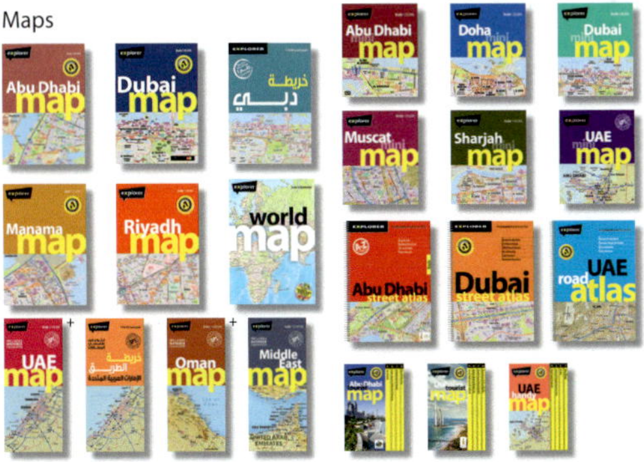

Adventure & Lifestyle Guides

Apps & eBooks

+ Also available as applications. Visit askexplorer.com/apps.

* Now available in eBook format.

Visit askexplorer.com/shop for a full product list.

explorer

Explorer Team

Check out askexplorer.com

Publishing

Chief Content Officer & Founder
Alistair MacKenzie

Editorial

Managing Editor Carli Allan
Editors Andy Mills, Kirsty Tuxford, Laura Coughlin
Deputy Editors Lily Lawes, Stacey Siebritz
Production Coordinator Rahul Rajan
Editorial Assistant
Amapola Baldo
Researchers Amrit Raj, Roja P, Praseena, Maria Luisa Reyes, Suzzette Privado, Shalu Sukumar

Design & Photography

Creative Director Pete Maloney
Art Director Ieyad Charaf
Layout Manager Jayde Fernandes
Senior Graphic Designer Gary McGovern
Junior Designer M. Shakkeer
Cartography Manager Zain Madathil
Cartographer Noushad Madathil, Dhanya Nellikkunnummal, Ramla Kambravan, Jithesh Kalathingal
GIS Analyst Aslam
Photographer & Image Editor
Hardy Mendrofa

Sales & Marketing

Director of Sales Peter Saxby
Media Sales Area Managers Sabrina Ahmed, Bryan Anes, Louise Burton, Matthew Whitbread, Laura Zuffova
Business Development Manager
Pouneh Hafizi, Nischay Kaul
Corporate Sales Manager
Zendi De Coning
Director of Marketing Lindsay West
Senior Marketing Executive
Stuart L. Cunningham
Director of Retail Ivan Rodrigues
Retail Sales Coordinator
Michelle Mascarenhas
Retail Sales Area Supervisors
Ahmed Mainodin, Firos Khan
Retail Sales Merchandisers Johny Mathew, Shan Kumar
Retail Sales Drivers Shabsir Madathil, Najumudeen K.I., Sujeer Khan
Warehouse Assistant Mohamed Haji, Jithinraj M

Finance, HR & Administration

Accountant Cherry Enriquez
Accounts Assistants Sunil Suvarna, Jeanette Enecillo
Administrative Assistant
Joy San Buenaventura
Reception Edelyn Isiderio
Public Relations Officer Rafi Jamal
Office Assistant Shafeer Ahamed
Office Manager – India Jithesh Kalathingal

IT & Digital Solutions

Digital Solutions Manager Derrick Pereira
Web Developer Mirza Ali Nasrullah
IT Manager R. Ajay
Database Programmer Pradeep T.P.

Contact Us

Website
Check out our new website for event listings, competitions and information on your city, and other cities in the Middle East. Log onto ask**explorer**.com

Newsletter
Register online to receive Explorer's weekly newsletter and be first in line for our special offers and competitions. Log onto ask**explorer**.com

General Enquiries
We'd love to hear your thoughts and answer any questions you have about this book or any other Explorer product. Contact us at info@ask**explorer**.com

Careers
If you fancy yourself as an Explorer, send your CV (stating the position you're interested in) to jobs@ask**explorer**.com

Contract Publishing
For enquiries about Explorer's Contract Publishing arm and design services contact contracts@ask**explorer**.com

Maps
For cartography enquiries, including orders and comments, contact maps@ask**explorer**.com

Advertising and Corporate Sales
For bulk sales and customisation options, for this book or any Explorer product, contact sales@ask**explorer**.com

Useful Numbers

Abu Dhabi Municipality	800 22220
Emergency	999
UAE Country Code	971
Abu Dhabi Area Code	02
Al Ain Area Code	03
Directory Enquiries (du)	199
Directory Enquiries (Etisalat)	181

Airport Info

Etihad Airways	02 599 0000
Emirates Airline	600 555 555
Abu Dhabi International Airport:	
Help Desk	02 505 5555
Flight Information	02 575 7500
Baggage Services	02 505 2771

Taxi Companies

Al Ghazal Taxi Abu Dhabi	02 444 7787
Al Ghazal Taxi Al Ain	03 751 6565
Arabia Taxi	02 558 8099
Cars Taxi	02 551 6164
Emirates Taxi	02 550 9511
Emirates Taxi Al Ain	03 782 5741
National Taxi	02 554 2231
National Transport Company	02 672 5656
Tawasul Taxi	02 673 4444
Tawasul Taxi Al Ain	03 782 5553
Trans AD	600 535353